REMEMBER JESUS CHRIST

Remember Jesus Christ

Believing the Absolute Truth about the Absolute Person in a Relativistic Age

Published by Founders Press
P.O. Box 150931 • Cape Coral, FL • 33915
Phone: (888) 525-1689
Electronic Mail: officeadmin@founders.org
Website: www.founders.org

Printed in the United States of America

ISBN: 978-1-943539-59-8

REMEMBER JESUS CHRIST

BELIEVING THE ABSOLUTE TRUTH ABOUT THE
ABSOLUTE PERSON IN A RELATIVISTIC AGE

THOMAS J. NETTLES

Contents

Preface

The theme of the 2024 Founders Conference surrounds Paul's admonition, "Remember Jesus Christ, risen from the dead, the offspring of David, as preached in my gospel" (2 Tim. 2:8 ESV). God willing, and according to His enlightenment and strength, I want to discuss this sobering theme by focusing on the biblical developments of "remember." The word points to events that are both pivotal and central. Not only do those events alter the direction for humanity, but they rise to a culmination and a subsequent response in thought and deed. The flow of the entire biblical text presses forward to this command: "Remember Jesus Christ."

"Remember" calls to mind central admonitions in the history of God's revelation of redemptive power to His people. The command is not for a mere mental recall of an event or a casual reminder of a person's name or status. It is a critical summons to put an event or person or commitment so at the center of your concern that the weight of its importance transforms your thinking. When the thief said to Jesus,

"Remember me when You come into your kingdom" (Luke 23:42), he wanted to be taken personally by Jesus into that status of perfect, sinless, beneficent rulership. Jesus responded with an answer commensurate with the purpose of the request, "Assuredly, I say to you, today you will be with Me in Paradise" (Luke 23:43). It is as though the Lord were saying, "As surely as My work of atonement will bring Me into the glory of heaven in the presence of the Father, so it will do for you." The request of the crucified thief was for Jesus's personal investment in the eternal well–being of his mind, body, and soul—"remember."

"Remember the Sabbath day, to keep it holy" (Ex. 20:8) involves not just simple mental recall, but also an investment of life in the rhythm of divine labor. As God worked for six days in creation, so should these redeemed people labor for six days at life–sustaining tasks that deserved their energy. As God finished creation and then rested, so were the people rescued from relentless labor in Egypt to embrace a Sabbath as instituted and practiced by God on the seventh day. All the animals, each member of the family, all the nation would so esteem the glory of the Creator/Redeemer/Covenant God that their lives, individually and corporately, would be defined by it. "Remember Jesus Christ" has that same claim on the lives of His redeemed ones, but with an even greater intensity in light of an even more powerful delivery.

In Genesis 9:15, God said to Noah that He would "remember My covenant" made with the whole earth never again to destroy all flesh by flood. At the appearance of the rainbow in the cloud (which God Himself makes), "I will look on it to remember the everlasting covenant between God and every living creature" (Gen. 9:16). God's promise to remember reflects a decree set in the context of His own integrity, a promise made by the God who does not lie (Titus 1:2).

In Leviticus 26:42 and 45, God referred to remembering His covenant with Abraham and Isaac so that He would not destroy the people entirely when they go into captivity: "I will remember the covenant of their ancestors, whom I brought out of the land of Egypt." When God remembers, He conducts Himself in accord with His eternal decree to redeem sinners through a man who would come in the context of a nation and a family, a man whose genealogy is traceable to Abraham and to Adam. The theology of "remember" means that God's purpose and consequent action of redemption captures the mind and determines actions.

Deuteronomy 6:12 gave a stern warning: "lest you forget the LORD who brought you out of the land of Egypt." God provided a formula for protection against their fatal forgettings. Generation upon generation should follow this system of instruction.

> And these words which I command you today shall be in your heart. You shall teach them diligently to your children, and shall talk of them when you sit in your house, when you walk by the way, when you lie down, and when you rise up. You shall bind them as a sign on your hand, and they shall be as frontlets between your eyes. You shall write them on the door-

posts of your house and on your gates. (Deut. 6:6–9)

The whole life should be lived in the conscious awareness of God's authority, His commands, His sovereign mercy, the fearful wonder of His distinguishing grace. The words of revelation that He has given, by which the meaning of His historical acts of grace are disclosed, must be an ever–present body of informative truth to His people. We must not forget; it must not pass away from our consciousness that we are saved by free, unmerited, sovereign mercy.

Deuteronomy 8 verses 2, 11, 14, 18, and 19 have an antiphonal chorus that works between the seriousness of the command to remember and the devastation wrought by the tragedy of forgetting. "And you shall remember" (v. 2) refers to the Lord's provisions and testing in the forty years of wilderness wanderings. This was to focus their lives and their hearts on the revealed Word of God as the source of life (v. 3). Should temporal blessings make them flatter themselves with a sense of independence, they were warned not to "forget the LORD your God" (11) and ignore His commandments. Again verse 14 warned against allowing success in the Promised Land to push aside the obvious dependence that they had on the Lord, even as it was undeniable during the testing of the forty years. If they were tempted to say, "My power and the might of my hand have gained me this wealth" (v. 17), they again were commanded, "You shall remember the LORD our God, for it is He who gives you power to get wealth, that He may establish His covenant which He swore to your fathers" (v. 18). "Remember" challenges the mind to grasp the covenantal mercy of God with such conscientious commitment that nothing can drive a wedge of temporal delusion between the moral and spiritual mind of a person and the infinite power and mercy of divine provision.

When Jesus established the symbol of the final, ultimate, perfect redemptive act, He commanded His followers, "Do this in remembrance of Me" (Luke 22:19). When Paul recounted the event for the Corinthians, he connected Jesus's command of remembrance with the breaking of the bread and the taking of the cup. "This do, as often as you drink it, in remembrance of Me" (1 Cor. 11:24–25). Paul added that such an action was a proclamation of "the Lord's death till He comes" (1 Cor. 11:26).

The command of Paul to Timothy to "remember Jesus Christ," therefore, reaches deep into the biblical text as a prompt to take to heart the covenantal faithfulness of God. "Remember" means to be in active reflection on the saving mercy contained in the eternal covenant and the consequent redemptive action of God in Jesus Christ.

Introduction

Paul was designated as a steward to "make the word of God fully known" (Col. 1:25 ESV). "Fully known" meant two things. One, Paul would preach and write without omitting any truth revealed to him. Two, it meant that when the stewardship of this mystery reached its final revealed proposition by those appointed to receive it, it would be complete; it would not come short of anything of revelatory status. This calling laid great demands on Paul. "It is required of stewards that one be found trustworthy" or faithful (1 Cor. 4:2 NASB). Paul had not invented this message or been an entrepreneurial religionist, but he was arrested by God, compelled as it were to this work. "Woe is me if I do not preach the gospel!" (1 Cor. 9:16).

Though he called the gospel "my gospel" in the text that drives this book (2 Timothy 2:8) and other places, he did not mean that he dreamed it or deduced it or commenced

1

it, but only that the revelation he himself received is the only gospel and there is no other (Gal. 1:6–12). Paul did not have the option to pick parts of the revelation and leave others behind. He must be a steward of all the essential elements of the gospel: born of woman and Son of God, hell and heaven, repentance and assurance, cross and crown, obedience and grace, incarnation of humility and second appearing in glory. During Paul's life, he made the word of God full through his preaching. The last verse of Acts views Paul in his rented house in Rome "proclaiming the kingdom of God and teaching about the Lord Jesus Christ with all boldness and without hindrance" (Acts 28:31 ESV). Collaterally, his situations called for writing letters to churches and persons. In those he reiterated his spoken ministry, and the written manifestations of his message took on the stature of Scripture, the written word of God (1 Thess. 2:13; 5:27; 1 Tim. 6:2b–3, 20; 2 Tim. 1:13–14; 3:10, 14–16; 2 Peter 3:15–16).

Paul preached truths that were hidden in the past from others (Col. 1:26). He emphasized that what was now preached with clarity and conviction formerly was a "mystery." He wrote the same in Romans 16:25, saying that the preaching of Jesus Christ came according to "the revelation of the mystery kept secret" but has been manifested now. Religious philosophers that lurked among the people spoke much of their mysteries and sought to lead people astray. Their so–called mysteries were lies and delusions, products of their own philosophical imaginations. The apostolic revelation of the mystery pointed to a person, Jesus Christ, who had appeared in the flesh in a specific time and space and fulfilled in His own body all the expectations of the prophetic writings.

Paul proclaimed Christ. Though the doctrines surrounding Christ form a beautiful system of theology, it is useless and of no account if it does not ultimately arise from and conform to the fullness of who Christ Himself was and is. "Remember Jesus Christ," Paul said in our driving text. In Paul's proclamation of Christ, his focus concentrates on the person of the Lord Himself and the work He did that He was uniquely qualified to do. This is a shorthand way of saying that Paul concentrated on the necessary relationship of law and gospel. Though our conduct should reflect righteousness as defined in God's law, we fall short, we are under condemnation, and we need rescue from the power of darkness (Col. 1:13). We need one who is qualified to perform such a rescue, and that is found only in Christ, the beloved Son of God who, by His righteous labors, has given us both redemption and the forgiveness of sins (Col. 1:13–14). No marvel, therefore, that Paul would remind Timothy in the context of such absolute consequences, "Remember Jesus Christ."

Not only did Paul labor to the point of agony (Col. 1:29) to secure a clear view of this infinitely glorious person, but he also suffered as if he were a criminal (2 Tim. 2:9). To the Colossians, he wrote that he rejoiced in his sufferings. It was the necessary consequence of his accurate impassioned presentation of the gospel of Christ. The world is offended by its moral implications on the one hand (i.e., that we are all sinners and deserve hell) and on the other hand holds a snobbish sense of intellectual skepticism concerning its leading affirmation (i.e., that God became man and died in the place of hell–deserving sinners). Paul's conversion, his suffering, and his absolute confidence of the revealed truth of his gospel should give serious pause to any person tending to dismiss Paul's articulation of the path to "eternal glory" (2 Tim. 2:10). Even beyond the evidence for the absolute credibility of Paul, we find the imposing uniqueness of Jesus Christ and His resurrection from the dead as justifying the words of the apostles, "Lord, to whom shall we go? You have the words of eternal life, and we have believed, and have come to know, that you are the Holy One of God" (John 6:68–69 ESV).

"Remember Jesus Christ risen from the dead, the offspring of David, as preached in my gospel, for which I am suffering" (2 Tim. 2:8 ESV).

1

Remember the Name of Jesus Christ

JESUS AS MESSIAH, PROPHET, PRIEST, AND KING

"Remember Jesus Christ, risen from the dead, the offspring of David, as preached in my gospel" (2 Tim. 2:8 ESV). In supplying the name of the one we are to remember, this passage also supplies the reasons that forgetfulness in this matter is fatal. Paul named the person who embodies the full range of truth and saving grace that counters the falsehoods, errors, and aggressive evil of fallen humanity. As he reminded the Corinthians, "As in Adam all die, even so in Christ all shall be made alive" (1 Cor. 15:22). In the context of the letter to Timothy, Paul used the combination "Christ Jesus" or "Jesus Christ" fourteen times. Two of these also employ the word "Lord" with the name, "Jesus," and the office, "Christ." Also, there are fifteen other uses of the word "Lord" to refer to Jesus Christ. The book is saturated with Jesus Christ—His lordship, His mercy, His purpose, His truthful word, His conquering of death, His promise of life, His salvation, His status as judge, and His personal presence with the believer. Paul aimed to make it impossible to forget either the person or the work of Jesus Christ. To forget is to deny; to deny is to give surety of an absence of grace.

In particular, Paul did not want us to forget the significance of the name and the title given to Him. His name is *Jesus*. The angel told Joseph, calling him "son of David," that the child with whom Mary was impregnated by the Holy Spirit was to be called "Jesus" (Matt. 1:20–21). The significance of this designated name was related to the child's office as Savior—"for He will save His people from their sins." The name means "Jehovah is salvation."

For Joshua (the same name) in the Old Testament, his name was a testimony to the promise of Jehovah in giving to Israel the land of Abraham. It signified that Jehovah was strong, mighty, faithful, the only God, and that He would accomplish all His promises, both of blessing and of cursing. He would work through Joshua to fulfill these promises and establish the context where the people would respond to this miraculous deliverance and strikingly clear revelation. Some of the promises were unconditional and unilateral. No alterations among the Israelites could change the ability and determination of God to carry through. Others were conditional and were, in one sense, dependent on the faithfulness of the people (2 Kings 23:26–27).

The task of Joshua was typological; the task for Jesus was

substantive and absolute. Joshua set the stage for the power-ful display of divine purpose; Jesus embodied the mystery of godliness. Joshua testified of the power of God to save and called the people to follow him in serving the Lord (Josh. 24); Jesus did not merely testify to the power of God to save, but He possessed and executed His saving power by His own righteous acts and perfect obedience. Not only did Jesus, like Joshua, testify to the power of God to save, but He constitut-ed the saving purpose of God. Though "Jesus" is His human name, it also is a testimony to His divine nature—"Jehovah is salvation."

As *Christ*, the God–man Jesus is the anointed one. Every office and type established by anointing the Christ culminat-ed in Himself. Did God give prophets to reveal and speak and write His Word to His people? Jesus is the prophet promised through Moses (Deut. 18:15, 18), the Word made flesh (John 1:14), the Son through whom God has spoken (Heb. 1:2). Is He not the true Elisha, the God of supplica-tion, anointed by Elijah (1 Kings 19:16; Luke 1:17; 3:21–22; Luke 23:34; John 1:29–34). Does the Lord not set forth the prophet as a special representative of His anointing? "Do not touch My anointed ones, and do My prophets no harm" (1 Chron. 16:22; Ps. 105:15). Does not Jesus claim that He is the fulfillment of the anointed prophet sent to preach good tidings to the poor, and proclaim liberty to the captives (Isa. 61:1; Luke 4:18)?

Jesus is priest. As the Levitical priest was anointed to of-fer sacrifice (Lev. 4:4–5) and sprinkle the blood of the sacrifice, Christ offered Himself once–for–all, putting an end to all of the typological sacrifices. Though not of the tribe of Levi, He received a special commission for this purpose (Heb. 7:20; 8:6; 9:12, 24–26). So Jesus Christ, having served as the anointed prophet, then completed His anointed work of priesthood, altar, and sacrifice. Nothing in the sacrificial system was left unfulfilled by Him.

Jesus is king. David was anointed king by Samuel (1 Sam. 16:13). In consequence of the Christ's completed prophetic work and the perfection of His priesthood, He was given His seat "at the right hand of the Majesty on high" (Heb. 1:3), fulfilling the promise to David of the forever king established by God. "And I will establish him in My house and in My kingdom forever; and his throne shall be established forever" (1 Chron. 17:14). Jesus Christ alone, in all three of His offices, can say, "I have been anointed with fresh oil" (Ps. 92:10).

Nothing else would matter if the next phrase in 2 Timothy 2:8 were not vital to the way we are called upon to remember Jesus Christ. Both the soteriological power and the apologetic coherence of the gospel would fall to the ground, no more to rise, without it. "Risen from the dead" denotes the conquering of the scheme of Satan to oppose the purpose of God in lifting up non–angelic creatures to a position higher than the angels—in fact, to share in some way with the glory of His Son. Jesus did not give aid to angels but was "made like His brethren" and made "propitiation for the sins of the people" (Heb. 2:17), and having "purged our sins" (1:3), destroyed "him who had the power of death, that is, the devil"

(2:14). The wages of sin, the penalty of death for disobedience, unpropitiated through the ages, held as a threat by the devil and verified by divine justice, lost its sting when Jesus "bore our sins in His own body on the tree" (1 Peter 2:24). Jesus Christ, who bore those death–dealing sins, was "raised from the dead by the glory of the Father" (Rom. 6:4). This means that all the holy, righteous, and just attributes of God, the entire weightiness of God, were honored completely by Christ's death and thus called for the granting of life to the successful sin–bearer. Death, therefore, no longer has any hold on Christ or His people, and Satan's tool of intimidation has been removed. The work of Christ and the verdict of the Father are communicated in power to the redeemed by the Spirit. "If the Spirit of Him who raised Jesus from the dead dwells in you, He who raised Christ from the dead will also give life to your mortal bodies through His Spirit who dwells in you" (Rom. 8:11). God, therefore, instead of being against us is for us. Why? Because He "spared not his own Son, but delivered him up for us all" (Rom. 8:32 KJV). Having given us His Son, He freely gives us all that Christ has gained. None can now condemn, for "it is Christ who died, and furthermore is also risen, who is even at the right hand of God." On top of that He "makes intercession for us" (Rom. 8:34).

Under the name of Christ, we have already looked briefly at the significance of the phrase "the offspring of David," or "out of a seed of David." The use of *spermatos* without the definite article means that the word "seed" does not identify Jesus as *the* seed of David (though that surely follows) but means that Jesus's birth was "out of (*ek*) a seed of David," that is, his mother Mary. Jesus was conceived in and then born from Mary, a seed of David. Luke 1:27 has the phrase 'of the house of David," which is to be applied both to Mary and to Joseph. The seed of the woman (Gen. 3:15) was also the seed of David. He descended from David in His human nature and has a right to the throne. "He will be great," the angel told Mary, "and will be called the Son of the Highest. And the Lord God will give Him the throne of His father David" (Luke 1:32). How low the House had fallen that a teenage virgin was to bear the seed of David, the Messiah, and His legal father would be a mere carpenter. Luke 2:4 again emphasizes that Joseph was "of the house and lineage of David" because the enrollment must take place legally according to the male of the household. When the angel addressed Joseph to inform him of the source of Mary's impregnation, he called him "Joseph, son of David" (Matt. 1:20). Jeremiah 30:9 predicts that "they shall serve the LORD their God, and David their king." In Ezekiel we read, "David My servant shall be king over them" (37:24). Hosea predicted that, after a time of devastation, Israel would "seek the LORD their God, and David their king" (Hos. 3:5). This descent from David confirms the prophetic material concerning the Messiah, seals the reality of His humanity, and shows that the true "Man after God's own heart" saves us and rules over us with lovingkindness until the kingdoms of this world become the kingdom of our Lord and of His Christ.

2

Remember the Gospel of Jesus Christ

The gospel was no matter of human construction, nor a philosophy to be shaped by critical interaction. It was not Paul's gospel in the sense that he deduced it from a clever, or even a profound, integration of secular cultural ideals. He did not invent it nor construct it by logical extension from his thorough knowledge of the Old Testament Scriptures. His gospel was indeed the culmination of the Holy Scriptures and the perfect and intended fulfillment of their meaning in historical narrative, prophetic utterance, typological events and persons, wisdom literature, and worship material. He told Timothy that the "Holy Scriptures . . . are able to make you wise for salvation through faith which is in Christ Jesus" (2 Tim. 3:15). Those Scriptures, which Timothy had been taught from childhood by Lois his grandmother and Eunice his mother, were to be seen in their perfect meaning when he viewed them in light of "the things which you have learned and been assured of, knowing from whom you have learned them" (2 Tim. 3:14). Paul referred to his own instruction, for Timothy had "carefully followed my doctrine" (2 Tim. 3:10). What Paul called "my doctrine" here, he had called "my gospel" a few paragraphs earlier.

In Romans 1, Paul began describing his ministry, indeed his authority, to the Romans as "a bondservant of Jesus Christ, called to be an apostle, separated to the gospel of God" (1:1). He then summarized this gospel in terms virtually synonymous with 2 Timothy 2:8, as that "which He promised before through His prophets in the Holy Scriptures, concerning His Son Jesus Christ our Lord, who was born of the seed of David according to the flesh, and declared to be the Son of God with power according to the Spirit of holiness, by the resurrection from the dead" (Rom. 1:2–4). Then he added the particular idea we are considering, that it is Christ through whom "we have received grace and apostleship" (1:5), or, perhaps, "this particular grace of apostleship." Paul went on to say, in light of the large Gentile mixture in the church at Rome, that his purpose was "to bring about the obedience of faith for the sake of his name among all the nations" (1:5). As Paul closed Romans, he told the church that God "is able to establish you according to *my gospel* and the preaching of Jesus Christ" (Rom. 16:25, emphasis added). His gospel was the "revelation of the mystery kept secret since the world began" (16:25). Though kept hidden as to the kind of person who could fulfill all the requirements of prophecy, who could judge justly and yet forgive sins and remove them as far as the east is from the west, in that revelation it was "made manifest" (16:26). Then, in a way perfectly consistent with the Scriptures of the prophets, this gospel that he called "my gospel" was "made known" to the nations.

Similarly, to the Ephesians Paul wrote that "grace was given, that I should preach among the Gentiles the unsearchable riches of Christ" (Eph. 3:8). The gospel that he preached carried the authority of his apostleship, his independent understanding of the gospel of Christ revealed to him: "that by revelation He made known to me the mystery" (Eph. 3:3). As he told Timothy, this gospel now constitutes a part of the Holy Scripture (2 Tim. 3:16) and brings all of its parts into perfect harmony. By the gospel, certain mysteries that lingered in the prophets were given clarity. Peter referred to this in 1 Peter 1:10–12, asserting that "those who have preached the gospel to you by the Holy Spirit sent from heaven" gave clarity to both "the sufferings of Christ and the glories that would follow." Mysteries left buzzing in the heads of the prophets found their resting place in "Jesus Christ, risen from the dead, the offspring of David, as preached in my gospel." Paul went on to tell the church in Ephesus about his "insight into the mystery of Christ" that was not made known in previous generations but "has now been revealed to his holy apostles and prophets by the Spirit" (3:4–5 ESV). Of this gospel, God's powerful grace made Paul a minister, a steward of the revealed truth concerning "the unsearchable riches of Christ" (3:7–8).

When among the church at Corinth false teachers came

who taught that there is no such thing as a resurrection of bodies, Paul began his instruction with a strong assertion of the absolute truthfulness of the gospel that he had preached. By his gospel they would be saved; if his gospel was not true, their faith would be empty. Note how insistent he was on the certainty of his message. To counteract these heretics, Paul reviewed "the gospel which I preached to you" and asserted the certainty of their salvation "if you hold fast that word which I preached to you" (1 Cor. 15:1–2). What did he preach? "I delivered to you as of first importance what I also received" (1:3 ESV). From whom did he receive this message that he preached? As Paul argued throughout his corpus of letters, he received it by divine revelation so that his gospel was for certain the gospel of God.

The first necessary theological truth is precisely this: preaching by an apostle. "We preach and so you believed. Now if Christ is preached that He has been raised from the dead, how do some among you say that there is no resurrection of the dead?" (1 Cor. 15:11–12). Preached, therefore believed. If taught otherwise than what was preached by an apostle, the message is false, even without further investigation. Other doctrinal ideas of major importance were eventually discussed—forgiveness of sins, the conquering of death, the reigning of the Man from heaven—but it is striking that the first thing Paul mentioned was the unity of the apostolic witness on this issue. Only a revelation could accomplish such unanimity.

If unalterably true, as Paul claimed, his gospel would

bear the scrutiny of critical examination in places where it touched on matters open to investigation. True belief, however, would arise in the context of the apostolic word, not the scrutiny. The resurrection of Christ and the consequent resurrection of believers were unambiguous facts of this divine revelation. The divine grace that captured Paul, making him an apostle, also confirmed to him the content of the gospel that he preached. His gospel, as revealed to him by the Holy Spirit, was a message of salvation grounded both in Scripture and in history. "Christ died for our sins according to the Scriptures" (1 Cor. 15:3). "Christ died" was historical; "for our sins" was theological, a matter of divine revelation and in perfect harmony with these prophetic words: "The LORD has laid on Him the iniquity of us all . . . He bore the sin of many" (Isa. 53:6, 12). "That He was buried" and "that He rose again the third day according to the Scriptures" related two historical facts that Paul proceeded to verify by historical evidence—multiple eyewitnesses of the risen Christ—including his own remarkable conversion and call to preach (1 Cor. 15:5–10). Then, with the historical evidence, he interwove truths of consistent biblical witness, including that the Lord Messiah would be seated at the right hand of the Lord "till I make Your enemies Your footstool" (Ps. 110:1). Also, He would come in power as the "Son of man, coming with the clouds of heaven" and would be given "dominion and glory and a kingdom" (Dan. 7:13–14). Only the resurrection of the crucified Messiah can explain such events.

In his letter to the churches of Galatia, Paul was shocked and amazed that someone could come among them preaching a supposed gospel other than what Paul preached and actually be credited as truthful. Paul had no room for suavity, politeness, or deference on this issue but said, in no uncertain terms, "Even if we, or an angel from heaven, preach any other gospel to you than what we have preached to you, let him be accursed" (Gal. 1:8). Why is Paul so certain of the correctness of his anathematization? "The gospel which was preached by me is not according to man. For I neither received it from man, nor was I taught it, but it came through the revelation of Jesus Christ" (Gal. 1:11–12). Paul had no doubts that his gospel was *the* gospel; he had no doubt that his gospel was the same as that preached by the other apostles; he had no doubt that he received his gospel by divine revelation.

3

Remember the Jesus Christ
of the New Testament

Having examined the theological importance of the call to "remember Jesus Christ," we want to examine some points of New Testament admonition in which the substance of the command is at work. As Jesus prepared His disciples for His departure, He promised them the help of the Holy Spirit. One operation of the Spirit that served the cause of redemption and the full truthfulness of the apostolic recording of it was couched in the promise of Jesus, "These things I have spoken to you while being present with you. But the Helper, the Holy Spirit, whom the Father will send in My name, He will teach you all things, and *bring to your remembrance* all things that I said to you" (John 14:25–26, emphasis added). The faculty of memory under the teaching of the Holy Spirit became the avenue for a theological and spiritual transformation. They had heard the words of Jesus, but none of the disciples grasped their meaning, and certainly not their world–transforming importance. But when the Spirit of truth came and brought these words to their "remembrance," the message was sealed in their thought, and its overturning power in an upside–down world became the theme of their lives and their hope of eternal life.

At the empty tomb we have the first post–resurrection call to "remember." When women arrived very early in the morning following the Sabbath and found the tomb empty, an angel said to them, "Remember how He spoke to you when He was still in Galilee, saying, 'The Son of Man must be delivered into the hands of sinful men, and be crucified, and the third day rise again'" (Luke 24:6–7). As they gazed into the empty grave where His body was laid, the angel asked them to gather the words of Jesus into their minds and to consider with their hearts that the dark emptiness they saw was in itself a settled and infallible proof of the truth of Jesus's words and the confirmation of His person and work. Had they remembered these words before the angel prompted them, they would have known what had happened. *Jesus has risen, just as He said. Death is conquered, sin is forgiven; eternal life is the unfading, immutable reality.*

When Paul wrote of his amazement that some in Galatia were "turning away so soon from Him who called you in the grace of Christ, to a different gospel" (Gal. 1:6), he expressed the result of a failure to remember Jesus Christ. When Paul wrote of being "crucified with Christ" and the results of that identity in death with Christ (Gal. 2:20–21), he was showing what it means to remember Jesus Christ. When he told the Galatians that "if you become circumcised, Christ will profit you nothing" (5:2), he showed what it means to remember Jesus Christ. If you remember Jesus Christ, the gospel is clear, the cross is dear, and the ceremonial law with its burdensome reminders—sin not yet atoned, hearts still in need of circumcision—will disappear.

When Paul closed his letter to the Ephesians with the benediction, "Grace be with all those who love our Lord Jesus Christ in sincerity" (Eph. 6:24), he highlighted the benefit of a remembrance of Jesus Christ. When he told the Philippians that neither endearment nor rivalry was of importance to him as compared to the greatness of the gospel, he remembered Jesus Christ. Paul expressed it this way: "What then? Only that in every way, whether in pretense or in truth, Christ is preached; and in this I rejoice, yes, and will rejoice" (Phil. 1:18). When Paul gave his extended and exalted expositions of the person and work of Christ in Colossians, he pressed those believers, "As you therefore have received Christ Jesus the Lord, so walk in Him, rooted and built up in Him and established in the faith, as you have been taught, abounding in it with thanksgiving" (Col. 2:6–7). This was a way of saying, "Remember Jesus Christ." And when he reminded them that all of the ceremonial law had been fulfilled and put to rest with the words "the substance is of Christ" (Col. 2:17), he was telling them that the answer to every challenge of philosophy and short–circuited theology is to remember Jesus Christ. When he told the Thessalonians to "stand fast and hold the traditions which you were taught, whether by word or epistle," (2 Thess. 2:15), he was saying, "Remember Jesus Christ." In demonstration of this, Paul went on to say, "Now may our Lord Jesus Christ Himself, and our God and Father, who has loved us and given us everlasting consolation and good hope by grace, comfort your hearts and establish you in every good word and work" (2 Thess. 2:16–17). To stand fast in those things handed down from the apostles is to find safety in Jesus Christ, for He has manifested saving grace in that the Father has given Him to us for comfort now and everlasting hope in the eternal future. What courage, conviction, and consolation is found in the gracious call, "Remember Jesus Christ"!

When Paul highlighted the extent of the saving grace of Christ, he told Timothy that "Christ Jesus came into the world to save sinners, of whom I am chief" (1 Tim. 1:15). Paul pointed to his saving confrontation with Christ as the pattern of how deep and infinitely gracious and powerful and certain is the determination of Christ to save, "that in me first Jesus Christ might show all longsuffering, as a pattern to those who are going to believe on Him for everlasting life" (1 Tim 1:16). Looking at his life and seeing its subjection to the one whom he persecuted, Paul was saying, "Remember Jesus Christ."

When John warned against false prophets, he gave this test: "By this you know the Spirit of God: every spirit that confesses that Jesus Christ has come in the flesh is from God, and every spirit that does not confess Jesus is not from God"

(1 John 4:2–3). By His revelation in a body when the eternal Word was made flesh (John 1:14), the eternally covenanted grace of God made the way for righteousness, forgiveness, resurrection, and glorification. Only "the man Christ Jesus" (1 Tim. 2:5) has done, or even could do, such deeds of grace and power. You have not remembered Jesus Christ if you do not remember that the incarnation was the sphere in which every redemptive act must of necessity be accomplished.

Jude went from writing an expressive exposition of the shared faith of Christians (Jude 3) to presenting a distilled warning against men of heretical doctrine and perverse lives. He told them, "Remember the words which were spoken before by the apostles of our Lord Jesus Christ" (Jude 17). In addition to their pursuit of all the "ungodly deeds" recorded in Scripture, a fatal doctrinal error undergirded their energy in turning the "grace of our God into lewdness;" that is, "they deny the only Lord, even our Lord Jesus Christ" (Jude 4). They denied the Lord because they did not remember "the words" previously spoken "by the apostles." Had they remembered, in the biblical sense of mental submission to the eternal truths of the covenant, they would have been warned of the perversity of unbelief and kept themselves "in the love of God, looking to the mercy of our Lord Jesus Christ unto eternal life" (Jude 21). How salubrious and safe is the command, "Remember Jesus Christ."

4

Remember Jesus Christ in Our Suffering

The Gospel Proceeds and Succeeds through Suffering

Paul's strong emphasis on the central points of Christ's person and work was designed to elevate the thinking of Timothy above the concerns for safety and acceptance in this life. We must remember—seeing the eternal covenantal purpose of God as centered on Jesus Christ—so that nothing in this life can draw us away.

One specific concern that Paul had was the power of physical and political intimidation to make us forget. He had already admonished Timothy not to be "ashamed of the testimony of our Lord, nor of me His prisoner" (2 Tim. 1:8). The "testimony of our Lord," in light of this context, could refer to the words of Jesus in Mark 8:38, where Jesus explained what is involved in denying oneself, or losing one's life for the sake of Christ, in order to follow Christ: "Whoever is ashamed of Me and My words in this adulterous and sinful generation, of him the Son of Man also will be ashamed when He comes in the glory of His Father with the holy angels."

That Paul has in mind physical persecution for the gospel as this challenge to the professing Christian is clear when he states that "I suffer hardship even to imprisonment as a criminal" (2 Tim. 2:9 NASB). His suffering was well–known by Timothy (3:10–11). Paul admonished him to "suffer hardship with me, as a good soldier of Christ Jesus" (2:3 NASB).

Paul had a two–fold purpose in referring to his various sufferings for "my gospel." One, his suffering sealed in his experience the absoluteness of the gospel. He was willing to lose all, including life, because of "the surpassing worth of knowing Christ Jesus my Lord. For his sake I have suffered the loss of all things" (Phil. 3:8 ESV). He even desired to know "the fellowship of His sufferings, being conformed to His death" (3:10). He was, in fact, at that moment contemplating that soon his life would be taken, for he knew that "the time of my departure is at hand" (2 Tim. 4:6). Nothing, therefore, could dissuade Paul from his clear and convinced proclamation of the finality, absoluteness, and consummate truthfulness that "Jesus Christ, risen from the dead, the offspring of David, as preached in my gospel." He had come to believe, embrace, and cast the very essence of his existence on the truth of the proposition that "the sufferings of this present time are not worthy to be compared with the glory which shall be revealed in us" (Rom. 8:18). If the former enemy, who was willing to imprison and kill those who believed the gospel, had changed so radically that he now gladly suffered imprisonment and the prospect of a martyr's death, who could doubt the certainty of his conviction? Who but the most irrational skeptic could deny the truth of Paul's message?

Second, Paul not only used his suffering to glory in the truth of the gospel, but also its power. The Word of God is not chained, imprisoned, or bound in any way (2 Tim. 2:9). The divinely ordained harmony in service of absolute sovereignty must be contemplated with reverence when we read, "For this reason I endure all things for the sake of those who are chosen, so that they also may obtain the salvation which is in Christ Jesus and with it eternal glory" (2:10 NASB). Elect in Christ in eternity past, saved in Christ in this present age, secured in Christ for undiminished joy for the eternal age yet to be. The gospel will not fail; it will prevail, and its power will be manifest in the faithful suffering of His people. Even in the face of heresy, Paul can affirm, "Nevertheless the solid foundation of God stands, having this seal: 'The Lord knows those who are His'" (2:19).

The gospel proceeds into the world through suffering, succeeds through suffering, and gives power to endure suffering. The gospel certainly will succeed, and Christ will lose none of His sheep; not one for whom the Shepherd has died will fail to enter the sheepfold. But such certainty arises and is perfected in suffering. Christ suffered and died, the blood of the martyrs is the seed of the church, and believers will choose eternal life in Christ even in the face of the threat of death for believing. "How unworthy it is," Calvin proposed, "that we should think more of the fleeting life of this world than of the holy name of the Son of God"[1]

Paul summarized this amazing integration of certainty secured through endurance by means of a confession or hymn called a "faithful saying," used in the apostolic church to teach this truth. It had a memorable pattern of rhyme and rhythm in Greek. Responses and results of true belief were set in parallel with responses and results of faithlessness to Paul's gospel. The one whose faith arises from the electing purpose of God endures; the one left to his own faculties will wilt under pressure. To paraphrase 2 Timothy 2:11–13:

> If together with Him we die, also together with Him we live.
>
> If we endure the load, we will also reign with Him.
>
> If we shall deny Him, also that very one He will deny.
>
> If we prove to be without faith, He remains faithful.
>
> For to deny Himself he is unable.

Dying with Christ refers to His propitiatory substitution for His people and implies their willingness to share His earthly suffering. Being atoned for objectively and suffering experientially means that we attain the resurrection of the just. The other points of the confession naturally follow. It ends with the strong affirmation of the unperturbed eternal decree of God and the immutable truthfulness of His threats toward unbelief.

This hymn also is reminiscent of the words of Jesus when He commissioned and instructed the Twelve prior to their mission, including warnings about persecution: "Whoever confesses Me before men, him I will also confess before My Father who is in heaven. But whoever denies Me before men, him I will also deny before My Father who is in heaven" (Matt. 10:32–33). Jesus's words were meant for the hearer and the preacher, one of whom was Judas. Remarking on this passage in 2 Timothy, Calvin wrote, "His threat is directed to those who from terror of persecution give up their profession of Christ's name."[2]

In discussing this passage with a PhD student from SBTS, Michael Carlino, he sent me the following response after looking at both the language and the entire theological context of the hymnic confession. I found his remarks helpful and faithful to the text.

> It would seem irresponsible exegetically to suggest that God will be faithful to the faithless by granting salvation in [2 Timothy 2:13], because Paul is explaining in 13 why God is just and good in denying the apostate. For God to not deny the one who doesn't endure/denies him, would be for God to deny his own character/nature. And it would then take away from the glory of verse 11, which promises

that those who share in Christ's sufferings will indeed reign with him. For, if God can deny himself and grant salvation to the apostate, the elect who endure unto death have no confidence in God's trustworthiness. In other words, Paul is teaching that God's denying of the apostate flows from God's immutable character, just as the assurance of God's receiving of his saints flows from God's immutable character.

Those who are apostate—those who fall away from what they have professed—have never had the root of the new birth. That heaven-wrought transaction shifts the affections from the world to the glory of God as seen in Christ. Something else—arising from threat, covetousness, intellectual fascination, or flattery—has shown that their most abiding affection is for the world and not Christ. Paul assures us that "He who has begun a good work in you will complete it until the day of Jesus Christ" (Phil. 1:6).

Again, we see what a pervasive and existentially profound theological admonition Paul gave in saying, "Remember Jesus Christ, risen from the dead, the offspring of David, as preached in my gospel."

5

Remember the True Jesus Christ

Paul's alarm at the gullibility of the Corinthians in receiving false teachers arose from the implications this had for several issues of vital truth, all of which impinged on the genuineness of their faith. One, their undiscerning spirit questioned the authenticity of his appointment as an apostle. Could these false teachers relativize Paul's apostleship, they would do the same to his preaching. Paul, therefore, spent chapters 11 and 12 of 2 Corinthians demonstrating the genuineness of his apostleship in order for them not to be "led astray from a sincere and pure devotion to Christ" (2 Cor. 11:3 ESV).

A second issue concerned the nature of the spirit, or Spirit, at work in them. Receiving the message of these false apostles would mean that they did not believe by the work of the

Holy Spirit but actually had been duped, even as Eve was, by Satan disguised as an angel of light. John gave a succinct statement concerning the work of the Holy Spirit in relation to true belief when he asserted, "Whoever believes that Jesus is the Christ is born of God" (1 John 5:1). Third, if they received the alternative being offered to them and departed from Paul's gospel, then they had a different gospel, which, as he told the Galatians, is no gospel at all. Contrary to the claims of these false apostles, messengers of the great deceiver, what they toyed with had no saving power.

A fourth difficulty enveloped all the others. Such a shift in their religious persuasion would finally mean that they received "another Jesus whom we have not preached" (2 Cor. 11:4). Another gospel and another Spirit means another Christ, for the Spirit is given by Christ and the gospel is defined absolutely in terms of the person and work of Christ.

As argued earlier, the admonition to "remember Jesus Christ," with the parameters established concerning His person and work, implies a comprehensive commitment to a large range of doctrinal ideas. The unshakeable confidence that Paul had in the absolute authority of his gospel inhabits the words "whom we have not preached." We find both on the pages of the New Testament and in the history of the church a number of ways in which the Pauline exhortation to "remember Jesus Christ" had been disobeyed. Usually this amounted to a denial of some element of Christ's person and a consequent modification of His work and, thus, a severe alteration of the gospel preached by Paul.

One way that Jesus is forgotten is by a denial of His true humanity. John confronted this error when he said, "The Word became flesh and dwelt among us" (John 1:14). He also had in mind a group that hesitated to embrace the apostolic teaching of the full humanity of Christ when he assured the readers of 1 John that the very one who was from the beginning "we have seen with our eyes" and "looked upon and have touched with our hands" (1 John 1:1 ESV). To add strength to this doctrine, John said, "The blood of Jesus Christ His Son cleanses us from all sin" (1 John 1:7). Paul's concern about the nature of the spirit at work in tempting the Corinthians to believe on a Jesus whom he had not preached was joined by John when he stated, "By this you know the Spirit of God: Every spirit that confesses that Jesus Christ has come in the flesh is of God, and every spirit that does not confess that Jesus Christ has come in the flesh is not of God. And this is the spirit of the Antichrist" (1 John 4:2–3). As he observed the developments among those who desired to find a position of teaching in Christian congregations, John warned that they should watch themselves "so that you do not lose what we have worked for." Specifically, he referred to the "many deceivers" that had "gone out into the world" who "do not confess the coming of Jesus Christ in the flesh" (2 John 7–8 ESV).

The writer of Hebrews, after a clear exposition of the deity of Jesus (Heb. 1:1–13) and a warning about ignoring "such a great salvation" (Heb. 2:1–4), showed the ontological necessity of the true humanity of Christ. "He who sanctifies and those who are sanctified all have the same nature" (Heb.

2:11, my translation). Again he wrote, "Since therefore the children share in flesh and blood, he himself likewise partook of the same things" (Heb. 2:14 ESV). Then further, as he argued concerning the necessary qualifications of one who is to redeem fallen humanity: "Therefore he had to be made like his brothers in every respect, so that he might become a merciful and faithful high priest in the service of God, to make propitiation for the sins of the people" (Heb. 2:17 ESV). Unless He were like us—that is, a man of full human nature, corruption of soul excepted—He could not make propitiation for the sins of the people.

Likewise, Paul argued in a number of places that Christ's work of reconciliation would be impossible apart from the reality of the Son of God taking a real human nature to Himself when He was "found in appearance as a man" (Phil. 2:8). In that way "He humbled Himself and became obedient to the point of death" (2:9). And in Paul's instructions to the church in Colossae, he reminded them, "And you, who once were alienated and enemies in your mind by wicked works, yet now He has reconciled in the body of His flesh through death" (Col. 1:21–22).

Peter joined the apostolic chorus in celebrating the condescending grace of God in sending His Son to take our human nature to perform the work of redemption. Peter affirmed that sinners are "ransomed . . . with the precious blood of Christ" (1 Peter 1:18–19 ESV). He intensified this strong assertion with the words, "Christ suffered for us . . . who Himself bore our sins in His own body on the tree" (1 Peter

2:21, 24). All that we are in our bodies, Jesus became; if not, none of our race would find God's wrath and expectation for righteousness covenantally fulfilled.

We must take time to admire and adore the great display and wisdom, power, and mercy found in the confession, "risen from the dead, the offspring of David" (2 Tim. 2:8 ESV). None can explain, but only believe, the marvel displayed when the angel told Mary, "That Holy One who is to be born will be called the Son of God" (Luke 1:35). The one who slept in the boat and sweat great drops of blood also forgave sins, silenced demons, and said, "I and the Father are one." Come, let us adore Him.

6

Remember Jesus Christ
as Taught by Clement

CLEMENT OF ROME WROTE TO COUNTER
FALSE TEACHING IN THE EARLY CHURCH

Possibly the earliest post–Pauline, post–apostolic literature we have is in the letter of Clement of Rome to the Church in Corinth. Most likely this was written around AD 95–96, when persons appointed by the apostles still held office in the church but were being pressed out of leadership by a younger generation. Clement wrote, "For we see that you have removed certain people, their good conduct notwithstanding, from the ministry which had been held in honor by them blamelessly."[3] Clement lamented that because of one or two persons, the ancient church of the Corinthians was "rebelling against its elders," thereby heaping "blasphemies upon the name of the Lord" and by their "stupidity" creating danger for themselves.[4]

In order to counter this egregious violation of Christian fraternity and even apostolic authority, Clement reached deeply into the theology of the Bible, as seen most clearly in the condescension of Christ, to encourage that church to correct their error. In the process of his argument, we find evidence of strong development of a comprehensive biblical theology and trinitarian theology and the centrality of Christ's having assumed human nature to bring to fruition the eternal purpose of God toward His elect. The reality of the full human nature of Christ is one of the fundamental assumptions of the argument. A creedal orderliness is present in the structure and content of this letter.

The basic trinitarian structure of the implicit creed, surrounded by certain affirmations of the peculiar operations of each person of the Trinity, may be seen in several passages in Clement's sober and stately style. Clement countered the church's pride by calling attention to examples of great humility in Scripture, punctuating the entire discussion with Christ's example. The emphases on Christ's work in His human nature are prominent. Formerly, in the early days of the church, not only were they blessed with an "abundant outpouring of the Holy Spirit," but they gave heed to Christ's words, stored them in their hearts, "kept his sufferings before your eyes."[5] Again, to counter a recent surge of haughty self-importance, "Let us fix our eyes on the blood of Christ and understand how precious it is to his Father."[6] Clement looked at Rahab's scarlet thread as "making it clear that through the blood of the Lord redemption will come to all who believe."[7] He quoted Isaiah 53:1–12 as an illustration of his observation that "the majestic scepter of God, our Lord Jesus Christ, did not come with the pomp of arrogance or pride . . . but in humility, just as the Holy Spirit spoke concerning him."[8] He then summarized his point by saying, "If the Lord so humbled himself, what should we do who through him have come under the yoke of his grace?"[9]

Clement urged peace and harmony in the church because peace and harmony are "especially abundant to us who have taken refuge in his compassionate mercies through our Lord Jesus Christ." Again, Christ in His humanity has become the guarantee that God's purpose of blessing His people will certainly come to fruition: "Let us consider, dear friends, how the Master continually points out to us the coming resurrection of which he made the Lord Jesus Christ the firstfruit when he raised him from the dead."[10] Looking at Jacob as a man of blessings, Clement affirmed, "From him comes the Lord Jesus Christ according to the flesh."[11] Our salvation is, in fact, "Jesus Christ, the High Priest of our offerings, the Guardian and Helper of our weakness."[12] In encouraging and commending love as the cement for true fellowship, harmony, and humility in the church, Clement again pointed to the condescension and love of Christ in taking our nature to gain for us what we lost in our foolish pride: "Because of the love he had for us, Jesus Christ our Lord, in accordance with God's will, gave his blood for us, and his flesh for our flesh, and his life for our lives."[13] Such a strong emphasis on substitution would be irrelevant, in fact impossible, apart from the Son of God's coming by true human birth in a true human nature.

Always resident in each argument of the centrality of Christ in His true fleshly suffering is a reminder of the trinitarian arrangement of gospel truth. "The apostles received the gospel for us from the Lord Jesus Christ; Jesus the Christ was sent forth from God. So then Christ is from God, and the apostles are from Christ. Both, therefore, came of the will of God in good order. Having therefore received their orders and being fully assured by the resurrection of our Lord Jesus Christ and full of faith in the Word of God, they went forth with the firm assurance that the Holy Spirit gives, preaching the good news that the kingdom of God was about to come."[14]

Knowledge of these things does not come through any private intuition but from the very oracles of God—"for thus says the Holy Word."[15] The apostle Paul already had written to this church about their tendency to factions—"Truly he wrote to you in the Spirit about himself and Cephas, and Apollos." Rather than being contentious toward one another, they should be "contentious and zealous" about the "things that relate to salvation." For these things "you have searched the Scriptures which are true, which were given by the Holy Spirit; you know that nothing unrighteous or counterfeit is written in them."[16] By them the church should know that only the ungodly thrust out the holy. As Clement multiplied the scriptural examples of God's blessings to the humble, and the close alignment that humility and holiness have with each other, he inserted, "For you know, and know well, the sacred Scriptures, dear friends, and you have searched into the oracles of God. We write these things, therefore, merely as a reminder."[17]

Clement regularly pointed not only to the voluntary humility of Jesus Christ for our salvation but to the final glory of Christ. The harmony of the entire creation shows God's goodness to all things, "but especially abundantly to us who have taken refuge in his compassionate mercies, through our Lord Jesus Christ, to whom be the glory and the majesty for ever and ever. Amen."[18] Election moves logically toward a display of Christ's glory: "This declaration of blessedness was pronounced upon those who have been chosen by God through Jesus Christ our Lord, to whom be the glory for ever and ever. Amen."[19] Clement included election, trinitarian *perichoresis*[20] as actuating the substance of faith, and biblical authority in a statement of Christ's salvation as an exhibition of the glory of the Father:

> For as God lives, and as the Lord Jesus Christ lives, and the Holy Spirit who are the faith and the hope of the elect, so surely will the one who with humility and constant gentleness has kept without regret the ordinances and commandments given by God be enrolled and included among the number of those who are saved through Jesus Christ, through whom is the glory to him for ever and ever. Amen.[21]

These issues were related again in a prayer of Clement that "the Creator of the universe may keep intact the specified number of his elect throughout the whole world, through his beloved servant Jesus Christ, through whom he called us from darkness to light, from ignorance to the knowledge of the glory of his name."[22] Clement closed a long prayer by again referring to Jesus Christ as the channel of glory to the Father: "You, who alone are able to do these and even greater good things for us, we praise through the high priest and guardian of our souls Jesus Christ, through whom be the glory and the majesty to you both now and for all generations and for ever and ever. Amen."[23] Finally, Clement glorified God who "chose Jesus Christ and us through him to be his own special people," looking upon such a relation as foundational to our being "pleasing to his name through our high priest and guardian Jesus Christ, through whom be glory and majesty, might and honor to him, both now and for ever and ever. Amen."[24]

Clement remembered Jesus Christ. He saw the incarnation of Christ, His taking to Himself our flesh and nature, as the model for all Christian humility and consequent unity. Jesus consummated the decree of election by shedding His blood as high priest and rising from the dead as the firstfruit for our redemption. Through Him, the elect will see and find infinite joy in an eternal vision of the glory of God.

7

Remember Jesus Christ
as Confessed in the Apostles' Creed

RESPONDING TO EARLY HERESIES
WITH THE "RULE OF FAITH"

What we find on the pages of the New Testament regarding the true humanity of Christ, and the concerns stated by the apostles for those who deny it, continued into the second and third centuries in a variety of forms of Gnosticism. Among other problems presented by Gnosticism, two embrace all the others. One, salvation supposedly came through intuitive knowledge resident within certain spiritual persons. Two, the world of matter is intrinsically evil and was generated by an inferior deity. Implications of these claims include a denial of the final authority of the written word of the apostles and a denial of the full humanity of Christ, particularly the redemptive work accomplished in His flesh. In short, Gnostics denied all that Paul included

41

in his admonition to "remember Jesus Christ, risen from the dead, the offspring of David, as preached in my gospel" (2 Tim. 2:8 ESV).

In response to the insidious influence of this dualistic mysticism, the post–apostolic church developed the "rule of faith." The various recensions of the rule of faith were eventually synthesized into a statement that most succinctly, clearly, and economically expressed universally received Christian truth known as the Apostles' Creed. The finalized text of the Apostles' Creed appeared in the work of Pirminius (d. ca. 753) in AD 750. Pirminius used the succinct outline of biblical assertions to give instructions in Christian doctrine and morals to recently baptized Christians. Its twelve articles, according to pious legend, were given in order by the twelve apostles, beginning with Peter and ending with Matthias. The creed is trinitarian.

> I believe in God, the Father Almighty, Creator of Heaven and earth, and in Jesus Christ, His only begotten Son, our Lord: who was conceived by the Holy Ghost, born of the Virgin Mary, suffered under Pontius Pilate; was crucified, dead and buried: He descended into hell: the third day He rose again from the dead: He ascended into heaven, and sits at the right hand of God the Father Almighty; From thence He shall come to judge the living and the dead. I believe in the Holy Spirit, the holy catholic church, the communion of saints, the forgiveness of sins, the resurrection of the flesh, the life eternal. Amen.

One can see the immediate significance, in light of the claims of Gnosticism, of phrases such as "the forgiveness of sins, the resurrection of the flesh." What claims our energy presently are those phrases beginning with "and in Jesus Christ" and ending with "judge the living and dead." The affirmative sentences give a simple reflection of the facts of redemptive history as presented in biblical revelation. One can see that the focus on Christ's incarnation and redemptive labors in the human nature is of central concern. We find it in its incipient stage in the New Testament, but Gnosticism's denial of the true humanity of Christ had come to full flower.

Likewise, in the letters of Ignatius at the end of the first decade of the second century, we find a deep and clear commitment to trinitarian doctrine, the real humanity as well as true divine sonship of Jesus Christ, the efficacy of His true bodily suffering and resurrection, the person of the Holy Spirit, and the necessity of unity of doctrine in the church. Ignatius warned the church at Trallia to "partake only of Christian food, and keep away from every strange plant, which is heresy."[25]

"There is only one physician," Ignatius insisted, "who is both flesh and spirit, born and unborn, God in man, true life in death, both from Mary and from God, first subject to suffering and then beyond it, Jesus Christ our Lord."[26] Again, focused on the false teachers that presented Christ as a phantom–like creature, Ignatius proclaimed, "For our God, Jesus the Christ, was conceived by Mary according to God's plan, both from the seed of David and of the Holy

Spirit."[27] In writing to the Trallians, Ignatius gave evidence of a confessional formula similar to this creed. His language shows that he understood the trickery of the verbal circumlocutions used by heretics in seeming to exalt Christ while, in truth, they denied both His humanity and His eternal deity. Note how Ignatius sought to cut through their façade: "Be deaf, therefore, whenever anyone speaks to you apart from Jesus Christ, who was of the family of David, who was the son of Mary, who really was born, who both ate and drank, who really was persecuted under Pontius Pilate, who really was crucified, and died while those in heaven and on earth and under the earth looked on; who, moreover, really was raised from the dead when his Father raised him up, who—his Father, that is—in the same way will likewise raise us up in Christ Jesus who believe in him, apart from whom we have no true life."[28]

Throughout the writings of Justin Martyr (ca. 150) we find doctrinal assertions and phrases that show his familiarity with an early development of the "rule of faith" and his ability to apply those doctrinal principles in a variety of situations. For example, in his first Apology, Justin argued, "From all that has been said an intelligent man can understand why, through the power of the Word, in accordance with the will of God, the Father and Lord of all, he [the Word, or Son] was born as a man, was named Jesus, was crucified, died, rose again, and ascended into heaven" (Apology 46). Scattered throughout his Apology are phrases like these: "Jesus Christ our Savior was made flesh through the word of God, and took flesh and blood for our salvation." And also, "by the will of God he became man . . . he came as a man among men." In showing the truthfulness of the prophets, Justin narrated, "In these books, then, of the prophets we have found it predicted that Jesus our Christ would come, born of a virgin, growing up to manhood, and healing every disease and every sickness and raising the dead, and hated, and unrecognized and crucified, and dying and rising again and ascending into heaven, and both being and being called Son of God" (Apology 44). In his second Apology, Justin wrote, "For next to God [the Father], we worship and love the logos who is from the unbegotten and ineffable God, since also He became man for our sakes, that, becoming partaker of our sufferings, he might also bring us healing."[29]

So it is in the writings of Irenaeus (ca. 180), who, in writing *Against Heresies*, said,

> The church . . . received from the apostles and their disciples the faith in one God, the Father almighty, "who made heaven and earth, the sea, and all that in them is," and in one Christ Jesus, the Son of God, incarnate for our salvation, and in the Holy Ghost, who preached through the prophets the dispensations of God and the comings and the birth of the virgin and the passion and the resurrection from the dead, and the reception into heaven of the beloved, Christ Jesus our Lord, in the flesh, and his coming from heaven in the glory of the Father to sum up all things and to raise up all flesh of all mankind, that unto Christ Jesus our Lord and God our Saviour and King, according to the good pleasure of the invisible Father, "every knee should bow,

of things in the heaven, and things on earth, and things under the earth, and that every tongue should confess" him, and to execute just judgment upon all.[30]

In describing how in the person of Christ we discover both God and man, Irenaeus wrote, "His word is our Lord Jesus Christ who in these last times became man among men, that he might unite the end with the beginning, that is, Man with God."[31]

Later Irenaeus offered another summary, saying, "Our Lord Jesus Christ, the word of God, of his boundless love, became what we are that he might make us what he himself is." Irenaeus's description of Christ's incarnation shows how each stage of human life was sanctified by Him from infancy to adulthood. This led to his statement on recapitulation, which demonstrated how the unity of Christ's person in both natures, God and man, is essential.

> Therefore the Lord confesses himself to be the Son of man, restoring in himself that original man from whom is derived that part of creation which is born of woman; that as it was through a man that our race was overcome and went down to death, so through a victorious man we may rise up to life; and as through a man death won the prize of victory over us, so through a man we may win the prize of victory over death. . . . He has been united with his own handiwork and made man, capable of suffering. . . . He existed always with the Father; but he was incarnate and made man.

Tertullian (ca. 225), in his *Prescription Against Heretics*, put much confidence in the reception of "the rule of faith" that was given, at least in its essential content, by Christ Himself and proclaimed by the apostles, preserved in Scripture, and retained in the teaching of the apostolic churches. Tertullian did not waver in his conviction that "Christ laid down one definite system of truth which the world must believe without qualification, and which we must seek precisely in order to believe it when we find it." He went on to report that the rule of faith is

> that by which we believe that there is but one God, who is none other than the Creator of the world, who produced everything from nothing through his Word, sent forth before all things; that this Word is called his Son, and in the name of God was seen in divers ways by the patriarchs, was ever heard in the prophets and finally was brought down by the Spirit and Power of God the Father into the Virgin Mary, was made flesh in her womb, was born of her and lived as Jesus Christ; who thereafter proclaimed a new law and a new promise of the kingdom of heaven, worked miracles, was crucified, on the third day rose again, was caught up into heaven and sat down at the right hand of the Father; that he sent in his place the power of the Holy Spirit to guide believers; that he will come with glory to take the saints up into the fruition of the life eternal and the heavenly promises and to judge the wicked to everlasting fire, after the resurrection of both good and evil with restoration of their flesh.[32]

Augustine (ca. 421) used the order of the creed in writing

his *Enchiridion*, probably alternating between the version of Hippo and the version of Milan for precise wording. The creed served as the basis for several other writings and sermons. He pointed to the Lord's Prayer and the creed as easily memorized and constituting the sum of faith, hope, and love.

> Because the human race was oppressed with great misery because of sin, and stood in need of the divine mercy, the prophet foretold the time of God's grace and said *Then everyone who calls on the name of the Lord shall be saved* (Jl 2:32). That is the reason for the prayer. But when the apostle quoted this testimony of the prophet in order actually to proclaim God's grace, he immediately added *But how are they to call on one in whom they have not believed?* (Rom 10:14). That is why we have the creed.[33]

Having its basis in the biblical revelation of the Trinity and the focus on the work of Christ in His incarnation, these teachers shared the truth of the apostolic revelation that had Christ not been truly like us in all things pertaining to our humanity—the corrupting power of original sin excepted—He could in no sense be a redeemer of this race. Gnostics such as Valentinus sought to deny the true humanity of Christ, and Marcion sought to destroy the unity between the God of creation and the God of redemption, yet biblically sound Christian teachers found the creed's synthesized assertions helpful in exposing the faulty steps of heresy. They focused on the unity of Scripture, the unity of God, the truth and necessity of the incarnation, and the reality of Christ's fully redemptive death and resurrection accomplished in His human nature in indivisible unity with his eternal Sonship. The presence of the Holy Spirit, the unity of the church, the resurrection of the just and the unjust—and the reality of eternal states of each—gave biblical symmetry to the whole of the truths confessed. In order to defend, teach, and confess the truth as well as test its existence in others, this creed served the cause of orthodoxy well and still stands as one of the truly ecumenical expressions of biblical faith.

Those who saw the "rule of faith" as faithful to Scripture, who served in the development of this rule into the Apostles' Creed, did so in obedience to the Pauline admonition at the center of this book: "Remember Jesus Christ, risen from the dead, the offspring of David, as preached in my gospel" (2 Tim. 2:8 ESV).

8

Remember Jesus Christ
in His Deity

To remember Jesus Christ, we must affirm His deity. To reject the true eternal deity of this singular person is to deny Him and bring the consequence that He will deny us. The mysterious reality that the man, Jesus of Nazareth, was at the same time and in the same person the Son of God constitutes our redemption and the source of our eternal worship.

Twice Luke tells us that Mary kept certain things "in her heart." (Luke 2:19, 51). On the first occasion, Luke adds that she "pondered them." Both the events and the words that accompanied them were too large for immediate comprehension. But that she kept them in her heart means that she remembered them intensely; she sought expanded understanding of what had happened and what she had been told.

51

Not only deeper cognition was needed, but a spirit of adoration and worship fitting for the eternal wonder of the event.

As a virgin, she was told that the Holy Spirit would come upon her to impregnate her in order to bear a child that she would call Jesus (Luke 1:31). He would be called "the Son of the Highest" (1:32). She learned, therefore, that not only did the Holy Spirit make her pregnant with a child, according to her seed, to be established and nurtured in her womb, but the "Highest" Himself, God the Father, would overshadow her simultaneously with the Spirit's coming upon her. The result was that not only would the child conceived by the Holy Spirit in her womb be a man called Jesus, but as the result of the overshadowing of the "power of the Highest," the Holy One born to her would be called "the Son of God" (Luke 1:35).

Within the span of a few minutes, the leading mysteries of classical orthodoxy were present in the very body of Mary. The Trinity and the duality of natures in the single person of Christ were concentrated in a moment in the angel's announcement and in Mary's own body. The fulfilling powers of redemptive history operated in perfect harmony to assure that "her Seed" would bruise the head of the serpent (Gen. 3:15) and destroy "him who had the power of death" (Heb. 2:14). Paul said, succinctly, "But when the fullness of the time had come, God sent forth His Son, born of a woman, born under the law" (Gal. 4:4). Her womb was the location of the "fullness of the time," and Holy Spirit, Holy Father, and Holy Son all converged, as it were, "in a moment, in the twinkling of an eye," to bring into the world the Redeemer. This Redeemer could, and did, effect forgiveness, procure righteousness, rob Satan's fold, reconcile God and sinners, overthrow death as sin's boon companion, and fit His people for heaven. The glory of the Father would be most fully and beautifully expressed when "at the name of Jesus every knee should bow, of those in heaven, and of those on earth, and of those under the earth, and that every tongue should confess that Jesus Christ is Lord" (Phil. 2:10–11). Just as it was announced, the name "Jesus" would designate the Savior and Lord. His humanity in the womb of Mary was due to the Holy Spirit's impregnation of her seed; His deity as Son of God comes from the Most High's extension of His eternal generation of the Son onto this fertile egg; His singularity of person with a complex combination of natures came from the Son of God's condescension to take the form of a servant and be made in the likeness of men in Mary's womb, though eternally He was "equal with God" (Phil. 2:6–8).

Mary went to visit her relative, Elizabeth, who exclaimed, "Blessed are you among women, and blessed is the fruit of your womb! But why is this granted to me, that the mother of my Lord should come to me?" (Luke 1:42–43). This child was indeed the fruit of Mary's womb, a seed of David but also the Lord.

Mary's immediate response to the words of Elizabeth were, "My soul magnifies the Lord, and my spirit has rejoiced in God my Savior. . . . He has helped His servant Israel, in remembrance of His mercy" (Luke 1:46–47, 54). When John the Baptist was born, Zacharias saw this child as "the prophet of the Highest," the one who would "go before the face of the Lord to prepare His ways" (Luke 1:76). This birth of John was in concert with the coming birth of "a horn of salvation for us in the house of His servant David" (1:69). These events were the action of God "to remember His holy covenant, the oath which He swore to our father Abraham" (Luke 1:72–73). We remember Jesus Christ because God remembers His covenant. In remembering, we confess with the mouth and believe in the heart that the Person and the pre-ordained events by which we are "delivered from the hand of our enemies" allow us to "serve Him without fear, in holiness and righteousness before Him all the days of our life" (Luke 1:74–75).

When the shepherds heard the speech of the angel, they learned that a child just born in Bethlehem was "a Savior, who is Christ the Lord" (Luke 2:11). Without doubt, this was told to Mary by the shepherds. The accumulation of titles of deity for this child surely startled and puzzled her, but she believed them. "Mary kept all these things and pondered them in her heart" (Luke 2:19). Upon His presentation in the temple after the days of Mary's purification, Simeon, under the immediate direction of the Holy Spirit and anticipation that he would see "the Lord's Christ," took the child and called him the Lord's salvation, with the affirmation that the child would be a "light to bring revelation to the Gentiles, and the glory of Your people Israel" (Luke 2:30, 32). Upon hearing that, Joseph and Mary "marveled at those things which were spoken of Him" (2:33). Marveling, pondering, and keeping were necessary and helpful responses to events that were the fulcrum of time and eternity.

When He went to the temple during the week of Passover, at twelve years of age, He took the position of a teacher, staying there several days beyond the week. He had gathered a fascinated and amazed group of scholars and teachers around him, answering their questions. As His mother and Joseph approached Him, oppressed by worry at His whereabouts, He responded, "Why did you seek me? Did you not know that I must be about My Father's business?" (Luke 2:49). They were puzzled at the calmness and confidence of His demeanor and "did not understand the statement which He spoke to them" (2:50). In spite of not understanding the fullness of Jesus's meaning and how His actions in the temple could be His "Father's business," Mary "kept all these things in her heart" (2:51).

The "mystery of godliness" that "God was manifested in flesh" (1 Tim. 3:16) will never be exhausted of its wonder and mystery. It is infinite as an expression of wisdom; it is inexhaustible as a matter for worship now and in heaven; it is full as the substance of the covenant of redemption. The interpenetration of all the persons of the Trinity in their fitting personal operations and their singularity of purpose, power, essence, mind, and will is startling to the soul. These actions of God, with their ontological implications, press the intellect with its insufficiency in investigating the ways of God. But the "hope of eternal life" is filled to overflowing with the prospects of living in the presence of this God and of observing and participating in the praise and worship of the man Jesus Christ in the eternal glory of His deity and His work of redemption.

Remember Jesus Christ.

9

Remember Jesus Christ
as the Word Became Flesh

"In the beginning was the Word" (John 1:1). With these
words, John affirmed that the living Word of God—that
is, the Son of God—was there and the active agent of the
events that began in Genesis 1:1: "In the beginning." Genesis
goes on to say that "God created." John's assumption of the
language of the Genesis narrative indicates that this Word
was the God who created. This is reiterated in verse 3 when
John wrote with economy and force, "All things through
Him"—as the intermediate but co–equal agent carrying
out the full intention of the Father—"came into being, and
without Him came into being not even one thing" (1:3, my
amplified translation). This is stated again in verse 10: "The
entire created order with all of its symmetry, inter–relations, and reciprocal dependencies and attractions [*cosmos*]

through Him, as the intermediate and effecting agent, came into being" (my amplified translation).

The verb "was," the imperfect of *eimi,* is used three times in verse 1 and again in verse 2. It implies absolute continual existence. After showing that the Word is eternal and the God who created, John said that the "Word was with God." This is a strong phrase of association, meaning "face to face with God" and including a definite article to make it literally "*the* God." Such language identified another personal being who also is eternally divine, even as the Word is. Immediately John continued with another statement about the Word: "the Word was God." The word "God" here is not the identical person identified as "God" in the previous phrase but is Himself, in His essence, a person of the same nature as "the God" that He was, is, and will continue to be "with." A. T. Robertson said that this phrase "presents a plane of equality and intimacy."[34] The same phrase appears in 1 John 1:2, and Robertson called it "the accusative of intimate fellowship." Later John verbalized this relation as "in the bosom of the Father" (1:18).

Verse 2 reiterates the assertion of verse 1 in shorthand style. "He" (this one who has just been called God) "was" (having continuing eternal existence without a beginning) "in the beginning" (when everything that has a beginning began) "with God" (face to face in essential union with a distinct divine person whom we learn is the Father). The perfect bond of intimate communion between Son and Father is the Holy Spirit (John 15:26; 16:14–15).

Verses 4, 5, and 9 engage the idea of the Word being the source, not only of physical created light, but also of the inextinguishable rationality and inner–witness in men called the "image of God" (Gen. 1:26–27). As Jesus is the uncreated image of God (Col. 1:15), even the "brightness of His glory and the express image of His person" (Heb. 1:3), so humanity, by created constitution, bears God's image. The Son has created us as reflections of His own being. "In Him was life, and the life was the light of men" (John 1:4). As the Father, by eternal generation, has given to the Son to have "life in Himself" (John 5:26), so the Son has given us, by creation, life and light that is dependent upon Him. The "light" is the rational morality and heart–law of humanity. The Word eternally exists as the true light (1:9), and every person who is conceived (who comes into being in this world) receives at that point the divine image as communicated by the eternal Word, the eternal radiance of the divine glory.

Sin, however, has darkened our perceptions. Bearers of the light walk about in darkness and thus, though the light–giver was in the world, "the world did not know Him" (John 1:10). Even His covenant people who had the fathers and the covenants and the written law did not receive Him (1:11). Revelation of truth diminishes cognitive darkness but does not overcome the spiritual darkness of the soul. The personification of truth, light, faithfulness, glory, and grace came into the world and none of His image–bearers, not even His own covenanted people, received Him or knew Him.

Another divine operation, therefore, must open that heart

and the rationality, banish the darkness, and bring sinners of all sorts to belief. John asserted that this happens by another birth in which we become "children of God, . . . not from bloods, nor of a will of the flesh, nor of a will of man, but of God having been begotten" (1:13, my translation). Here John rejected the genealogical pedigree of the Jews, the power of the human will, and all the powers present in humanity as a result of natural birth. The sinful darkness and spiritual deadness over Jew and Gentile can only be overcome by a birth from above.

In this tight framework, John established the deity of the Word, the Word's operation in creation, and His face-to-face connection with "the God." Now the astounding mystery—this Word became flesh; He dwelt among men as a man. At the same time, He could not be absent of His eternal glory, but He did not exhibit the external form of that glory. The evidence of His deity was abundant, but its form was exhibited rarely.

Nevertheless, John claimed, "We beheld His glory, the glory as of the only begotten of the Father, full of grace and truth" (1:14). John saw works of power befitting only God, but the glory he referred to here is the glory resident in the eternal relation between the Father and the Son. If John's words did not arise from revelation, how else could he state these propositions with such certainty and in a didactic way? This kind of revealed insight into the historical phenomena experienced by the disciples was promised by Jesus when He said, "I still have many things to say to you, but you cannot bear them now. When the Spirit of truth comes, he will guide you into all the truth, for he will not speak on his own authority, but whatever he hears he will speak." Jesus then completed the trinitarian unity of knowledge and purpose by saying, "He will glorify Me, for He will take of what is Mine and declare it to you. All things that the Father has are Mine. Therefore I said that He will take of Mine and declare it to you" (John 16:12–15). Paul summarized by saying, "What no eye has seen, nor ear heard, nor the heart of man imagined . . . these things God has revealed to us through the Spirit" (1 Cor. 2:9–10 ESV). "In other ages," Paul claimed, the mystery of Christ was not made known "as it has now been revealed by the Spirit to His holy apostles and prophets" (Eph. 3:5).

Does this contradict John's claims in 1 John? John said, "That which was from the beginning, which we have heard, which we have seen with our eyes, which we have looked upon, and our hands have handled, concerning the Word of life . . . we declare to you . . . and these things we write to you that your joy may be full" (1 John 1:1, 3, 4). It is true that John saw all these things, heard the words of the Word, felt the flesh of the Word made flesh, and considered all this a sufficient demonstration of the actions, claims, and teachings of Jesus. For such clarity of perception of these transcendent, historically certain truths, however, John had to partake of a two–fold work of the Holy Spirit.

First, he was the recipient of the revelation Jesus promised from the Spirit. His assertions about the deity of Jesus were not guesswork nor the mere product of rational deduction from abundance of evidence. Though consistent with the evidence, John's propositions were revealed truth.

Second, he received the Spiritually generated true–seeing, true–tasting, true–hearing. He had experienced what Jesus said after the feeding of the five thousand: "It is the Spirit who gives life; the flesh profits nothing. The words that I speak to you are spirit, and they are life" (John 6:63). He had experienced not only the revelation of cognitive propositions (like Balaam in Numbers 23:1–12), but also the internal apprehension of the truth taught by the Spirit, unlike Balaam (Jude 11, 19). True believers will not believe antichristian lies that deny either the deity or the humanity of Christ, for they "have an anointing from the Holy One, and you know all things" (1 John 2:20). In reference to the particular knowledge of the Father and the Son, the Spirit anoints His chosen with that knowledge. Confirming this, John wrote, "But the anointing which you have received from Him abides in you, and you do not need that anyone teach you; but as the same anointing teaches you concerning all things, and is true, and is not a lie, and just as it has taught you, you will abide in Him" (1 John 2:27).

True belief consists of several constituent elements. First, the historical events effecting redemption must have taken place. "The Word became flesh and dwelt [or set Himself up as a tabernacle] among us" (John 1:14). He "bore our sins in His own body on the tree" (1 Peter 2:24) and "died for our sins" (1 Cor. 15:3). He was buried, but "now Christ is risen from the dead" (1 Cor. 15:20). Having made purification for sins, He has sat down at the right hand of the Father (Heb. 1:3).

Second, true belief accepts the meaning of these things as taught infallibly by revelation to chosen messengers (1 Tim. 2:5–7). Truth and error are divided along the lines of apostolic declaration and contrary opinion (1 John 4:5–6).

Third, true belief emerges with a restoration of the true light to the soul by the glory of Christ's gospel, by a spiritual application of the historical truth that Jesus appeared as God in the flesh and accomplished His assigned work of redemption. Those who don't believe have been blinded by Satan so that "the light of the gospel of the glory of Christ, who is the image of God" does not enlighten them (2 Cor. 4:4). On the other hand, those who believe are the recipients of an effectual operation of Christ Himself, "who commanded light to shine out of darkness" at creation (4:6). He does this through the Spirit (for in this work "the Lord is the Spirit") and "has shone in our hearts to give the light of the knowledge of the glory of God in the face of Jesus Christ" (3:17–18; 4:6).

We remember Jesus Christ when we affirm—on the basis of apostolic revelation, with a heart full of love and adoration, without a shadow of doubt—that the Word who was with the Father, and was Himself eternally of the essence of the Father, became flesh.

10

Remember Jesus Christ, the Great "I Am"

When John summarized the narrative of his gospel, he acknowledged a strategic selectivity to the signs performed by Jesus. His purpose was "that you may believe that Jesus is the Christ, the Son of God, and that believing you may have life in His name" (John 20:31). In fact, not just the signs but all that John recorded compels the reader to a confession that Jesus is Lord and God (20:28–29), peculiarly qualified to effect salvation for those whom the Father had given Him (6:39). John gave the historically observable evidence for the theological conclusion, "In the beginning was the Word, and the Word was with God, and the Word was God. . . . And the Word became flesh and dwelt among us, and we beheld His glory" (John 1:1, 14).

The signs—seven of them recorded by John—are works of Jesus that required omnipotent power and benevolent purpose. For those who saw them and understood, they should have concluded that God is with us and is working for our well–being. Jesus changed water into wine to salvage a wedding celebration (John 2:1–11). At that, His disciples believed. He healed an official's son with a spoken word from afar (4:46–54). At that, the official and his household believed. He healed a man who had been an invalid for almost forty years by telling him to "take up your bed and walk" (5:1–15). At that the Jews reviled him, especially as Jesus called God His Father, "making Himself equal with God" (5:18). The opposing Jews, understanding the implications of the Father/Son reference, began their contrivances to kill Him. He fed a multitude of five thousand men, plus women and children, by multiplying five loaves of bread and two fish to satisfy the hunger of all. At that, the people said, "This is truly the Prophet who is to come into the world" (6:5–13). In the presence of weather–beaten, frightened disciples, He walked through a stormy sea to comfort them and quiet the storm (6:16–21). At that, those in the boat worshiped Him and said, "Truly, You are the Son of God" (Matt. 14:33). For a man born blind, with the use of mud made from Jesus's saliva and water for washing, Jesus restored his sight, prompting the man's worship (John 9). Jesus's friend Lazarus, dead for four days, He raised from the dead by calling him forth by command. Beforehand, He prayed, showing that the purpose of this astounding sign was that those standing around would "believe that You sent Me" (John 11:42). He wanted to make sure that observers knew that He operated in perfect conjunction with the power and purpose of the Father. At that, "many of the Jews . . . believed in Him" (11:45). When Jesus assured Martha that Lazarus would be raised, she confessed, "Yes, Lord, I believe that You are the Christ, the Son of God, who is to come into the world" (11:27). These signs identified Jesus as the one who told Moses, "I will do marvels such as have not been done in all the earth, nor in any nation" (Ex. 34:10).

John also recorded seven times that Jesus stated metaphors using the ontological identity for God, "I am." In doing so, He set Himself forth as the one in whom safety, life, sustenance, and eternity are secured. Jesus said, "I am the bread of life, "the light of the world," "the door of the sheep," "the good shepherd," "the resurrection and the life," "the way, the truth, and the life," and "the true vine" (John 6:35; 8:12; 10:7, 14; 11:25; 14:6; 15:1). John recorded Jesus's use of "I am" on five other occasions without any metaphorical reference (6:20; 8:24, 28, 58; 18:5). Both the metaphorical and absolute use of "I am" identified Jesus as the God who created all that is in the world and by whose word light was separated from the darkness. He is the one who protected and fed Israel in the wilderness; He is the true David, killer of the giant Death and the eternally reigning king. As the vine, He embodies Israel, the true man of God. As the Good Shepherd, He is the gate through whom they enter the fold; He calls them by name, and He died in order to secure eternal life for them. He was the ransom and the Redeemer for Job by whose power believers will, in their flesh, see God (Job 19:25–27; 33:24–25). His person and work exclude the possibility of any other person, philosophy, or religious system leading to a knowledge of the Father, but demonstrate that His way is infallibly certain.

Jesus identified Himself with no equivocation, no embarrassment, no apology, no mollifying explanation as the one who identified Himself to Moses as "I am" (Ex. 3:14). What astounding connections must have trammeled the pedestrian thoughts of the people as one stood among them who identified Himself to Moses by that name—"I am that I am; I eternally exist; I am unchangeable; I alone have non–dependent existence; it is to me that all moral beings, of all times, from all places will answer in final judgment." His claim meant that he was, therefore, "The Lord, the Lord God, merciful and gracious, longsuffering, and abounding in goodness and truth, keeping mercy for thousands, forgiving iniquity and transgression and sin, by no means clearing the guilty, visiting the iniquity of the fathers upon the children and the children's children to the third and the fourth generation" (Ex. 34:6–7).

Jesus told His detractors, "Do not think that I shall accuse you to the Father; there is one who accuses you—Moses, in whom you trust. For if you believed Moses, you would believe Me; for he wrote about Me. But if you do not believe his writings, how will you believe My words?" (John 5:45–47). Moses wrote about the Creator, the righteous Judge, the covenant maker, the God of Abraham, the God of deliverance, the Great Lawgiver, the angry God, the compassionate God, the God who reveals His glory, the God whose justice cannot be violated, the God who makes a way of forgiveness. Jesus was saying, *I am that God.*

The discourses recorded by John give Jesus's interpretation of confrontations of varying intensities with increasingly bold claims. In His discussion with Nicodemus, Jesus called Himself the Son of Man "who came down from heaven" and gives eternal life to believers (John 3:13–15). To the woman of Samaria, Jesus told her plainly concerning the identity of Messiah, "I who speak to you am He" (4:26). In a discourse with hostile Jews, Jesus enraged them even further by saying that the Father has committed all judgment to the Son, "that all should honor the Son just as they honor the Father. He who does not honor the Son does not honor the Father who sent Him" (5:23). Speaking in strong images about the necessity of His incarnation and death, Jesus again offended the grumblers by saying, "Most assuredly, I say to you, unless you eat the flesh of the Son of Man and drink His blood, you have no life in you" (6:53). In another discussion with the confused and increasingly agitated Jews, Jesus laid claim to a perfect knowledge of and conformity to the Father's purpose: "When you lift up the Son of Man, then you will know that I am He, and that I do nothing of Myself; but as My Father taught Me, I speak these things. And He who sent Me is with Me. The Father has not left Me alone, for I always do those things that please Him" (8:28–29). In His Good Shepherd discourse, Jesus said, "My Father, who has given them to

Me, is greater than all; and no one is able to snatch them out of My Father's hand. I and My Father are one" (10:29–30). When that claim prompted an effort to stone Him immediately, He pointed to their irrationality in disconnecting His words from His works, and continued, "Though you do not believe Me, believe the works, that you may know and believe that the Father is in Me, and I in Him." (10:38).

Identity in deity while maintaining distinction of personhood was too big an idea to absorb but was perfectly consistent with the witness of the Old Testament. In the discourse given at the Lord's Supper, Jesus made several summarizing statements: "You call Me Teacher and Lord, and you say well, for so I am" (John 13:13). "He who receives Me receives Him who sent Me" (13:20). "Now the Son of Man is glorified, and God is glorified in Him" (13:31). "I am in the Father and the Father in Me" (14:10–11). "He who hates Me hates My Father also" (15:23). "[The Holy Spirit] will glorify Me, for He will take of what is Mine and declare it to you. All things that the Father has are Mine" (16:14–15). "Blessed are those who have not seen and yet have believed [that I am Lord and God]" (20:29).

John saw and heard these things, testified to these things, and wrote these things. He remembered Jesus Christ and, under the superintending purpose of the Holy Spirit, recorded with the same revelatory value and infallible authority with which Paul preached his gospel.

11

Remember Jesus Christ as Confessed in the Nicene Creed

The first of the ecumenical creeds was formulated in a council called by the emperor Constantine. According to historians Eusebius of Caesarea and Lanctantius, Constantine was converted to Christianity as he prepared for a battle with Maxentius in the year 312. His victory, which he attributed to Christ, made him the sole ruler of the western portion of the empire. After a dozen years of gaining more knowledge of the church's organization and doctrines, Constantine, aware of a theological controversy that stirred the church, made arrangements for church bishops to meet in Nicea (present day Iznik in Turkey) to settle the dispute. Around three hundred bishops were able to come, with only half a handful of representatives from the west.

The controversy that prompted the call to Nicea focused on the teaching of a presbyter of Alexandria, Egypt, named Arius (260–336). Arius strongly concluded that the monotheism necessary to Christianity eliminated the possibility of any other personal entity sharing the status of absolute deity. In a letter to his friend Eusebius of Nicomedia in 318 during the initial tensions of the controversy, he complained that Alexander "greatly injures and persecutes us . . . since we do not agree with him when he says publicly, 'Always Father, always Son,' 'Father and Son together,' . . . 'Neither in thought nor by a single instant is God before the Son.'" Arius instead taught that "before he was begotten or created or ordained or founded, he was not." He, that is, the one called the Son, is not "a part of the unbegotten in any way" but was "constituted" by God's "will and counsel, before times and before ages."[35]

Arius's affirmation of the lordship of Christ, therefore, could not mean that He was co–eternal with the Father and of the same nature. The phrases anathematized at the end of the Nicene Creed 325 represent some of the phrases that Arius used to define his understanding of Jesus the Christ. For example, "Those who say, 'there was when he was not,' and 'out of nothing he came into being,' or 'he is of another substance or essence,' or 'the Son of God is created, changeable, mutable' are anathematized by the catholic and apostolic church."[36]

According to Arius, because only God is eternal, Jesus is not, and so, "There was when he was not." Since He is begotten, He must have come into existence subsequent to the Father and, therefore, "begotten" is taken as a synonym for "created." Since He is created, He cannot be of the same eternal immutable substance as the Father and is, on that account, of a different substance. Since He is a created moral being, even though the first of all created things, He is mutable and could have sinned. The Father, however, endowed Him with the power of creation and set Him forth to be the Redeemer of the fallen race, a task that the Son effected without blemish and thus gained the status of Savior. In order to be like us and succeed where we failed, He had to take our flesh. In His person, however, His humanity consisted only of the body while the created *logos* constituted the rational soul of the person Jesus.

This savior concocted by Arius, therefore, was neither God nor man. The views of Arius show that a single theological principle pressed with a relentless, but false, logic uninformed by other revelatory propositions leads to destructive conclusions.

Among the most important of the biblical theologians opposed to Arius was a young deacon at Alexandria named Athanasius (296–373). Athanasius had written a book entitled *On the Incarnation of the Word*. In it he had discussed how the incarnation of the Son of God solved an apparent dilemma. God intended to bring His creature, man, to a state of glorious fellowship with Him. He also threatened that if

His creature disobeyed then death would be the certain out-
come. How could God complete His purpose for man and
at the same time keep true to His word? The incarnation is
God's answer to this apparent dilemma. The one who was
both God and man could take the death man owed, for "all
men were due to die,"[37] thus fulfilling the veracity of God's
Word and the honor of God. At the same time, He brought
to glory the human nature that He shared with the creature,
thus fulfilling the divine purpose for man. Athanasius was
well–armed in biblical knowledge and in theological reflection for the vital corrective that the Arian speculation de-
manded.

Though the council had negative fallout in church–state
relations and the eventual authority of canon law, the most
important result out of Nicea was the adoption of the creed.
To show the pivotal importance of the substance of this creed
we will point to five short insertions. Eusebius of Caesarea
(the first church historian) proposed the confession used at
baptism by his church (or something very similar) as a possible statement to bring unity to the deeply divided council.
When the Arian party agreed to sign the proposed statement, the party led by Alexander of Alexandria (d. 328) and
his young deacon Athanasius knew that no real unity could
be gained by such a tactic. A creed that simply embraced
the serious doctrinal disagreements would only perpetuate
disharmony and lead to constant dispute. Ambiguity about
the legitimate object of worship would, in fact, endorse a
principle of idolatry and capitulate to the impression that
Scripture itself was not clear in its christological focus. The

wisdom of God would be impugned for leaving us without clarity on the status of the one He called "My beloved Son." What could be more absurd in Christianity than to leave the christological issue a matter of opinion, ambiguity, and diverse formulation?

Much of the clarification was attached to the phrase in Eusebius's confession "begotten from the Father." The first defining statement is in the words "from the substance of the Father." This means that the Son's existence is not an act of the will of the Father at a point outside His own eternity, as openly asserted by Arius. Athanasius contended, "Created things have come into being by God's pleasure and by his will; but the Son is not a creation of his will, nor has he come into being subsequently, as the creation; but he is by nature the proper offspring of the Father's substance."[38] The Son's co–eternality is intrinsic to the very existence of the Father as Father. If God's essential character is Father, then He could never be without His Son. One of the truths we know about God is His eternal paternity, and thus from that substance the Son eternally exists as Son.

A second defining phrase says that Christ is "true God from true God." Jesus was not inferior in His divinity; He was not constituted as a deity by dint of accomplishment nor granted the position or title as a reward for hard and faithful work. Because He was begotten of the substance of the Father, His deity is a true eternal deity, and His Sonship means that He is of the substance of His Father, truly divine. The Son of God is a true Son in the natural and moral image and likeness of his Father.

Third, the creed denied Arius's understanding of "begotten" by adding that Christ is "not made." The idea of begetting is a different reality from creating. That which is begotten shares the nature of the begetter. In his hard–hitting, intensely doctrinal, polemical refutation of Arianism entitled *Contra Arianos*, Athanasius pointed to the use of the term *begotten* in Scripture as sealing the reality that sons are of the same nature as their fathers. "The character of the parent determines the character of the offspring." Humans, as created, arise in time and beget in time and their begotten ones follow them in time, but they are not different in nature. "But the nature is one," Athanasius affirmed, "for the offspring is not unlike the parent, being his image, and all that is the Father's is the Son's."[39]

That sons follow fathers in time is not essential to the reality of begetting but only an accident of our state of being created and thus limited by time. That our children follow us in time does not mean they are of a different nature, but only that in creatures the process of begetting proceeds from generation to generation.

God, as a begetter, relates to His only begotten as Son to Father, sharing the same eternal attributes while also maintaining eternally distinguishing traits of personhood. For this reason, the doctrine of eternal generation was important to Athanasius. Never has there been any point in God's eternal existence when the Son was not begotten by the Father. If there had been, then the relation of Father and Son would be merely temporal, and there would be no way of maintaining a singularity in the divine essence while affirming a real plurality of persons. Without generation as an eternal operation of God, tritheism or modalism are the only alternatives.

The truth of eternal generation helps in the interpretation of certain passages of Scripture. For example, no doctrine gives greater aid in understanding John 5:26: "For as the Father hath life in himself; so hath he given to the Son to have life in himself" (KJV). Self–existence is an attribute of God only. The Father has this attribute necessarily and so that attribute distinctive of deity constitutes the self–existence of the Son, who is eternally generated by the Father. "In Him was life" (John 1:4). The Jews understood this ontological relationship of Father to Son to involve equality of essence. When Jesus called God His Father in a distinctive way, therefore, the Jews "sought all the more to kill Him, because He not only broke the Sabbath, but also said that God was His Father, making Himself equal with God" (John 5:18).

Fourth, the council adopted a controversial word to assure that none could interpret Christ's nature as inferior to or other than that of the Father in any sense. The word, *homoousios*—same essence, substance, nature—was controversial because it was used by a theologian named Sabellius in asserting that the essence of divinity has appeared in three modes as Father, Son, and Holy Spirit. Each of these manifestations is God, and, in sharing the same essence, are in reality only one Person. Modalism, as it was called, was heretical and prejudiced some of the concern against the word *homoousios*. The problem lay in the failure to define a difference between "essence" on the one hand, and "person" on the other. Tertullian (ca. 160–220) sustained the distinction in his Latin writings in deploying the terms *una substantia* and *tres personae*. His influence protected the West from the difficulty perceived in the mono–essentiality of Father and Son. In spite of the scary associations of the language among the Greeks, however, the creed affirmed that the Son is "of one substance with the Father." If He is begotten of the substance of the Father, ascertaining that He is "true God of true God" and that His begottenness can in no way be construed as createdness, then it is not only appropriate, but necessary, that the term *homoousios* be affirmed of the Son.

Fifth, in light of the strange anthropology of Arius, the creed attached to the phrase "was made flesh" the exegetical appositive "was made man." Arius believed that the only thing really human about Jesus was His flesh, and that His rationality was constituted by the created Word, or Son. When John wrote that "the Word became flesh and dwelt among us" (John 1:14), he never meant that Jesus had human flesh only without human mind, affections, or spirit. The phrase "made man" should not have been necessary to insert, but in light of the bizarre ideas of Arius, further definition was needed.

Note also the soteriological concern involved in this. It was in pursuit of "our salvation" that He took our humanity into His eternal Sonship. Had He, the eternal Son of God, not assumed our nature, He could in no wise be our Savior. He could not have lived for us in order to grant us His righteousness; He could not have died for us to bear our load of sin, guilt, and punishment. "The gift by the grace of the one Man, Jesus Christ, abounded to many" (Rom. 5:15).The Creed of Nicea is not Scripture and has no authority *as a creed*. Its synthetic arrangement of clearly biblical ideas, however, and its clarifying exegetical phrases give aid to the Christian in declaring with the mouth the esteem for and dependence on Jesus as Son of God and Savior that should be in the heart. This creed is a faithful expression of the announcement given by the angels at Jesus's birth: "For there is born to you this day in the city of David a Savior, who is Christ the Lord" (Luke 2:11). If we "remember Jesus Christ" with clarity, confidence, gratitude, and worship, we can recite these confessional affirmations from the heart.

This is my translation of the christological portion of the Nicene Creed of 325:

> We believe in one God, the Father almighty, maker of all things seen and unseen; And in one Lord, Jesus Christ, the Son of God, begotten out of the Father, only–begotten, that is, from the essence of the Father, God out of God, light out of light, true God out of true God, begotten not made, of one essence with the Father, through whom as an intermediary all things came to be, things in heaven and things on earth, who on account of us men and on account of our salvation came down, and was enfleshed even to

the point of true manhood, and suffered, and rose again on the third day, and ascended to the heavens, and will come to judge the living and dead.

12

Remember Jesus Christ as Son of God and Son of Man

The orthodox party of Nicea prevailed for less than a decade. Challenges to the Nicene formula soon began to multiply. For a brief period, Arianism was made the received doctrine of the empire.

Two other theological issues arose that called for closely reasoned biblical exposition. One concerned a construction of the human nature of Christ that compromised His full humanity by eliminating His human reason, human will, and thus all true human initiative. This was propounded by Apollinarius. His zeal for the deity of Christ and the necessity of His sinlessness and incorruptibility led him to deny that Jesus had a human soul.

Another issue concerned the person of the Holy Spirit. Was He a creature or was He, like the Son, of the same essence with the Father? Those who claimed the Spirit's works were the works of a creature were known as "fighters against the Spirit."

The Emperor Theodosius I called a council in 381 at Constantinople in order to reaffirm the theology embraced at Nicea fifty–six years earlier and to give closure to the controversy over the Holy Spirit and the humanity of Christ. The Creed of Nicea was reaffirmed with several phrases inserted to give clarity to the person and work of the Holy Spirit. We find, "By the power of the Holy Spirit he became incarnate from the Virgin Mary, and was made man." And also, "We believe in the Holy Spirit, the Lord, the giver of life, who proceeds from the Father [and the Son]. With the Father and the Son he is worshipped and glorified. He has spoken through the Prophets." The phrase "and the Son," *filioque* in Latin, was added to the Western version of this creed during the time of Charlemagne. It affirms the double procession of the Holy Spirit in eternity. The Spirit is, even as love flows eternally and personally between Father and Son, "the perfect bond of unity" (Col. 3:14).

Although the Constantinopolitan creed gave a measure of balance to affirmations concerning the persons of the Trinity and locked Arianism outside the pale of orthodoxy, it did not give a detailed synopsis of the relation of the uncreated (God) to the created (man) in the person of Christ. That the eternally generated Son of God had taken to Himself real humanity was now beyond dispute. The manner of this assumption of the human nature, however, and the appropriate words to use in asserting this truth, still seemed to elude a clear, biblically defensible, theologically sustained definition.

Nestorius, bishop of Constantinople, in response to a Mary–cult developing in his diocese, found it absurd to use the word *theotokos*, God–bearer, for Mary. He preferred the term *christotokos,* Christ–bearer. While firmly sustaining both the human and the divine, and conscientiously resisting the tendency to fuse, and lose, the human into the divine nature, Nestorius was perceived as erring on the other side. It seemed that he maintained such an individuality in the human nature that he treated the nature as a person. He viewed the union as only of undivided moral purpose, or a divine indwelling of the man born of Mary. His was a kind of high adoptionist Christology.

Cyril, bishop of Alexandria, kept the pressure on Nestorius, insisting that he anathematize the positions attributed to him. To make his position clear, Nestorious should affirm, "If anyone does not confess that Emmanuel is God in truth, and therefore the holy Virgin is *theotokos*—for she bore in the flesh the Word of God become flesh—let him be anathema."[40] Unable to consent to this anathema, Nestorius was exiled after the Council of Ephesus (431).

Cyril's language, however, gave rise to a group known as Monophysite (one nature) and Monothelite (one will). They contended that Christ, because of the infinite greatness of

His deity, had only one nature. The humanity was like a drop of honey absorbed into the ocean. In this vein of thought, Eutyches declared, "I confess that our Lord was of two natures before the union, but after the union I confess one nature."[41] This formula was resisted by Flavian, the bishop of Constantinople, and was condemned by a council in 448 that used the terminology of "two natures"—obviously protecting the full human nature—existing in the one Christ.

Eutyches, representing this as Nestorianism, with support from Theodosius II, called a synod in 449 composed of those who revered him and his theological instincts to approve his formula. Flavian's attempt to attend this council and provide a reasoned objection resulted in his being so grossly manhandled that he died. This synod soon was termed the *Latrocinium*, Robbers' Synod, by those who opposed Eutyches.

During the time of this theological, and sometimes physical, punch and counter–punch, the bishop of Rome, Leo, who was appealed to by both parties in this dispute, gathered enough information about what was at stake to weigh in with unusual clarity and vigor. Before Flavian's ultimate conflict, Leo wrote him concerning his view of the issue. This letter, so profoundly practical and biblical in its content, has gained a just commendation through the centuries. Known as Leo's *Tome*, its argument virtually sealed the issue concerning the relationship of Jesus's human nature and His divine nature in the single person. When a new council was called in 451 at Chalcedon to revisit the Eutychian problem, Leo's letter was read. Many of those in attendance greeted its reading with the words, "Peter has spoken." This should not prejudice those who reject the papal primacy or the Petrine succession of Rome against the power of the reasoning and synthesis of biblical truths present in this document. Edward Hardy wrote, "It is a fine specimen of the straightforwardness and clarity of the Latin mind—as also of the Western approach to the mysteries of Christianity from the facts of faith rather than the speculations of philosophy."[42]

Leo's reasoning from the commonly accepted confession of Christians and the biblical material concerning the incarnation of the Son of God is, in fact, tightly constructed and profound. The argument is Bible–centered and doctrinally coherent.

Leo said that if Eutyches "was not willing, for the sake of obtaining the light of intelligence, to make laborious search through the whole extent of the Holy Scriptures," at least he should have learned from the common confession, particularly the implications of its words, "His only Son, our Lord, who was born of the Holy Spirit and the virgin Mary." Failing that, he should submit to the implications of the gospel descriptions of the person and work of Christ, which show that "in the entire and perfect nature of very Man was born very God, whole in what was his, whole in what was ours," except for the corruption of sin.

As for the formula set forth by Eutyches ("out of two natures into one"), Leo indicated the greatest disdain. "I am astonished," he told Flavian, "that so absurd and perverse a profession as this of his was not rebuked by a censure on the part of any of his judges [in 448], and that an utterance extremely foolish and extremely blasphemous was passed over." Leo noted that it was just as impious to say that the only begotten Son of God "was of two natures before the incarnation as it is shocking to affirm that, since the Word became flesh, there has been in him one nature only."[43] How could two natures exist in the Son of God prior to the incarnation? Also, how could one who was not fully man as a result of the incarnation ever reclaim for humanity the moral image of the divine and the warrant to eternal life?

A method of biblical citation emerges in Leo's letter that helps the student of the Bible with an important principle of interpretation. His synthesis of texts employs a theological observation called the *communicatio idiomatum*—the fellowship of peculiar properties. This means that many texts in the Bible that would otherwise be confusing are perfectly clear when one sees the integrity of two natures in one person, Jesus Christ. Often Scripture asserts an action or attribute of one nature that, strictly speaking, holds true only for the other nature. Such is Paul's statement in Acts 20:28, "to feed the church of God, which he hath purchased with his own blood" (KJV). God does not have blood, but the person who purchased the church by His death did have blood and also was God. The same inference we draw from the words of Jesus in John 3:13: "No one has ascended to heaven but He who came down from heaven, that is, the Son of Man who is in heaven." Jesus had never been in heaven as Son of

Man, but as Son of Man He is the same person that as Son of God had come down from heaven. Even at that moment, as He spoke, as Son of Man united in person with the eternally generated Son of God, He was in heaven. Though He stood before Nicodemus, isolated in time and space by His body and by every property of His humanity—even as Nicodemus was—unlike Nicodemus, He also resided in heaven. The *communicatio idiomatum* gives the key to a proper grasp of such a text.

Sometimes Scripture will indicate a condition of the whole person that is true only of one nature (e.g., "Before Abraham was, I AM" in John 8:58). These kinds of texts are the seedbed for the theology of two natures in one person, and, once established, the theology becomes a principle of interpretation for a large number of texts. For example, in his famous *Tome*, Leo argued and illustrated that in this single person, "the lowliness of man and the loftiness of Godhead meet together." Though it does not belong to the same nature, it is true of the same person to say, "I and My Father are one" (John 10:30) and to say, "My Father is greater than I" (John 14:28). We find clearly stated the same mysterious truth in Paul's statement, "For had they known, they would not have crucified the Lord of glory" (1 Cor. 2:8). When Jesus asked who the *Son of Man* was, why does He commend the answer, "You are the Christ, *the Son of the living God*" (Matt. 16:16, emphasis added)?

Leo also kept pressing that the ontology of the person of Christ served the interests of the salvation of sinners "because one of these truths, accepted without the other, would not profit unto salvation."[44] It would be equally wrong, as well as dangerous to the soul, to believe the Lord Jesus to be God only and not man, or man only and not God.

At the time of the Olivet Discourse, Jesus made the puzzling affirmation, "But of that day and hour no one knows, not even the angels of heaven, but My Father only" (Matt. 24:36). Jesus, speaking by the Spirit and in His humanity, had been isolated from that knowledge. He could state with perfect accuracy and verity that, in His perfect manhood, the Son did not know what the Father had decreed concerning the coming in glory of the triumphant, risen, ascended, redeeming Son of Man. In His humanity, Jesus increased in wisdom. His knowledge and His perfect ability to apply it continually increased throughout His life as the man who was being perfected, that is, brought by degrees to a full and immutable righteousness (Luke 2:52; Heb. 5:8). This event was hidden even from Him in that peculiar capacity and at that time.

In his commentary on Matthew, John A. Broadus observed, "If there was to be a real incarnation of the Eternal Word, then the body he took must be a real body, and the mind a real mind. How his divine nature could be omniscient, and his human mind limited in knowledge, both being united in one person, is part of the mystery of the Incarnation, which we need not expect to solve."[45]

If Christ, in His perfection of moral rectitude and full

commitment to all that the Father willed, had this event hidden from Him at that time and yet trusted fully, even though He would go through the torturous propitiatory death, how willingly and joyfully should we submit to the mystery of our future with absolute trust in a faithful creator and Father. In this way, we "remember Jesus Christ" and emulate His submission to and trust in the Father's wisdom and will.

13

Remember Jesus Christ
as One Person with Two Natures

A SUMMARY OF THE CHALCEDONIAN CREED

Leo's *Tome* led to Chalcedon's clarity. The Chalcedonian Creed of AD 451 toes the line on the difficult idea of two natures maintaining absolute integrity with full manifestation of the distinct and incommunicable properties of each in one person. Also, for the first time in a creedal affirmation, we find the term *theotokos*—God–bearer, or mother of God. Often the term provokes an immediate negative reaction because of the truth that God is self–existent, without beginning, infinite in glory, power, and wisdom, dependent on nothing outside of Himself for His purpose, His decrees, or His ability to perform all that He so desires. The implications of Scripture are clear when He declares, "Who has directed the Spirit of the Lord, or as His counselor has taught Him? With whom did He take counsel, and who instructed Him, and taught Him in the path of justice? Who taught Him knowledge, and showed Him the way of understanding?" (Isa. 40:13–14). One would also pause before accepting such a doctrinally loaded word like *theotokos* because of specific affirmations of Scripture concerning the Son: "For by Him all things were created that are in heaven and that are on earth, visible and invisible, whether thrones or dominions or principalities or powers. All things were created through Him and for Him. And He is before all things, and in Him all things consist" (Col. 1:16–17).

So how can such a being ever be thought of as having a mother? This is precisely why Paul wrote, "And without controversy great is the mystery of godliness: God was manifested in the flesh, justified in the Spirit, seen by angels, preached among the Gentiles, believed on in the world, received up in glory" (1 Tim. 3:16). Though some manuscripts have the word "He," the grammatical context justifies the reading "*God* was manifested in the flesh." Paul wrote about "the church of the living God" (3:15)—or "the household of God" in the ESV—and begins the confession with the pronoun *hos*, translated "who," with "God" being the only antecedent.

This strange, but clearly revealed, truth of the birth of Christ shows that the conception by the Holy Spirit of the child in Mary was the moment of the union of God the Son with true humanity in one person who would be born, crucified, buried, risen, ascended, and so come again in like manner. As we discussed in a previous chapter, the mystery as announced to Mary was that she would "bring forth a Son" who would be given the "throne of His father David," and that He should reign forever and "of His kingdom there will be no end" (Luke 1:31–33). Though she knew not a man, this would happen because "the Holy Spirit will come upon you" (1:35), creating fertility in her egg without the corruption of a human father. At the same moment of such a conception, "the power of the Highest will overshadow you" (1:35). That means that the Father in His mysterious eternal activity of generating the Son caused a personal assumption of the human embryo by His Son with no lapse of time between the Spirit's work of conception, the Father's work of "overshadowing," and the Son's condescending to assume the human nature, committed to conduct Himself within the framework of humanity. That which was to be born of Mary would be called "the Son of God." The singularity of this person so conceived, therefore, would be God in the flesh—"And the Word became flesh and dwelt among us" (John 1:14).

This reality was revealed to Elizabeth, Mary's cousin, so that when Mary traveled to stay with her for some months, Elizabeth greeted her by saying, "Blessed are you among women, and blessed is the fruit of your womb! But why is this granted to me, that the mother of my Lord should come to me?" (Luke 1:42–43). These words of Elizabeth seem to confirm the rather startling title given to Mary in the Chalcedonian Creed. Among all the women of the earth, from the creation until the close of history, Mary was given this extraordinary blessing from God—though she knew the truth of the words "a sword will pierce through your own soul also" (Luke 2:35)—to be the one through whose seed the Messiah came. The real intent of such a title as *theotokos* and such an observation from Elizabeth was that this single child, this one person, enfleshed the Creator and sustainer of all that has been made as the one who also would be mediator between God and man, the man Christ Jesus.

Efforts to avoid the apparent clumsiness of the term "God–bearer" leads to erroneous assertions. To say "Mother of Christ" or "Christ–bearer" in order to avoid using the word "God" does not address the problem unless one is willing to assert that the Christ she bore was not God. If one seeks to avoid the hypostatic union of the two natures by saying the unity was only of sympathetic will, as the human person borne by Mary had established in His soul a complete union of purpose with the Son of God, then one is back to the error of adoptionism. The best option, given all the biblical data and the soteriological purpose of the incarnation, is to affirm the term *theotokos*, for it captures all the power implicit in the Johannine assertion, "The Word became flesh and dwelt among us."

On the basis of Leo's letter, therefore, the following paragraph was set forth by the council of Chalcedon as an explanation of the doctrine consistent with the Creed of Nicea.

> We, then, following the holy Fathers, all with one consent, teach men to confess one and the same Son, our Lord Jesus Christ, the same perfect in Godhead and also perfect in manhood; truly God and truly man, of a reasonable soul and body; consubstantial with the Father according to the Godhead, and consubstantial with us according to the Manhood; in all things like unto us, without sin; begotten before all ages of the

Father according to the Godhead, and in these latter days, for us and for our salvation, born of the Virgin Mary, the Mother of God, according to the Manhood; one and the same Christ, Son, Lord, Only–begotten, to be acknowledged in two natures, inconfusedly, unchangeably, indivisibly, inseparably; the distinction of natures being by no means taken away by the union, but rather the property of each nature being preserved, and concurring in one Person and one Subsistence, not parted or divided into two persons, but one and the same Son, and only begotten, God the Word, the Lord Jesus Christ, as the prophets from the beginning [have declared] concerning him, and the Lord Jesus Christ himself has taught us, and the Creed of the holy Fathers has handed down to us.[46]

When the council of Chalcedon met, a committee was appointed to finalize its statement of orthodoxy. They considered several documents that had been produced during the controversy between Cyril of Alexandria and Nestorius of Constantinople and the *Tome* of Leo concerning the position of Eutyches. The committee produced a document that succinctly and clearly stated the position of the council. Given the tensions present, and the fact that this was committee work, it is remarkable for its chaste conservatism, its doctrinal clarity, and its avoidance of metaphysical speculation. The pure "creedalism" of its assumptions, its anathemas, and its pretensions to virtual canonical status would probably be resisted by the free–church, *sola scriptura* orientation of Baptists and some others, but the careful expressions of the doctrine of Christ's person should be joyfully embraced as a lucid, profound, and biblically accurate guide to both doctrine and interpretive principles.

Several items of theological and interpretive importance are distilled in this short statement. First, the creed seeks the consent of the reader that this formula is a true presentation of Old Testament prophecy, the teachings of Christ Himself, the true doctrinal tradition of the church fathers, and the unalloyed meaning of the Nicene Creed.

Second, the creed recognized that Jesus Christ really was God incarnate, the second person of the eternal Trinity. The eternal Word who was with God (the Father) and was God (the Son) truly dwelt among men as a man. Jesus was not a mere phantom, nor a separately personed man adopted or merely inhabited, but the one whose scars, whose hands and feet, were those of the one who was Lord and God (John 20:28).

Third, the creed acknowledged Jesus the Christ as truly and fully human. Not only was His body of the same stuff as our bodies, but He had all the soulish, rational, and spiritual aspects of humanity, including human affections. His affections and perceptions constituted a soul that would be "exceedingly sorrowful, even to death" (Matt. 26:38). He was of the same essence ("consubstantial") as us but without the intrusive and corrupting factor of sin. Though people could clearly see that He was an extraordinary person (Matt. 16:13–16; Luke 7:14–17; John 3:2), none ever thought that He was less than a man.

Fourth, without any mixture or confusion of the two natures that would compromise the integrity of either, the creed held that Jesus was one person. All that He did as a person was an expression of the peculiar and distinguishing attributes of each nature. This perfect union in one person is emphasized by the vigorous expression of Mary as *theotokos* and the insistence that "the property of each nature" not only is preserved but concurs "in one Person." All that He did as prophet, priest, and king was done in His capacity of Christ, so that each nature, concurring in the one person, contributed essentially to the proper fulfillment of each office. For example, the First London Confession of the English Particular Baptists states, "That he might be such a Prophet as thereby to be every way compleat, it was necessary that he should bee God, and withal also that he should be man; for unlesse hee had been God, he could never have perfectly understood the will of God, neither had he been able to reveal it throughout all ages; and unlesse hee had been man, hee could not fitly have unfolded it in his own person to man."[47]

Fifth, the creed distinguished between nature and person. The personhood of Jesus was founded on the personhood of God the Son. The human nature was assumed by the Son of God but did not exist as a separate human person. This is where Nestorianism fell short of the doctrine of the hypostatic union, that is, this one single person who was born of Mary from the moment of conception and in every moment subsequent to His conception was both the eternal Son of God and the son of Mary, thus descended from David. This distinction between person and nature indicates that the properties of personhood are consistent, whether it be of God or man, while the natures are distinct. Those properties were consistent with Jesus's human nature expressing itself in a fully personal way, so that in His communications, friendship, and affections in His humanity, there was nothing that was impersonal.

Hallelujah, what a Savior!

Victories of the past do not suffice for the present. Champions of error will continually seek to reclaim ground that they have lost. Those who cherish the advances of truth from the past must seek to establish a bond with the courage, strength, and clarity of yesterday's captives of truth and uncorrupted worship. Each generation has an increasing burden, as well as blessing, of stewardship. Revelatory truths stated and defended through careful thinking, hard work, and wrenching conflict must not be lost. Contemporary challenges must be dismantled while the grounds of defense must be reclaimed. Implications for present issues and for further understanding of the richness of divine revelation becomes a part of the stewardship of those who desire to "continue in the faith, grounded and steadfast, and are not moved away from the hope of the gospel" (Col. 1:23) that they have heard, embraced, and found to be their very life.

14

Remember Jesus Christ as "A Ransom for Many"

CONSIDERING WHY JESUS HAD TO SUFFER AND DIE

To remember Jesus Christ necessarily involves a profound grasp of the reason for His death. This begs us to look unflinchingly into the phrase "risen from the dead" (2 Tim. 2:8 ESV). It is such a poignant and defining phrase, even offensive to rationality and common empirical observation, and it is a shockingly powerful distillation of the person and work of Jesus Christ. In searching for the purpose of Christ's death, we look first to Paul's reasoning toward some who denied that there would be a resurrection of the dead. Whether this denial was from the influence of Sadducees who were mingling with a Christian congregation (Acts 23:6–9), from specific philosophical influences to which the Corinthian church was vulnerable (1 Cor. 1:18–25), or from a proto–Gnosticism worming its way into the church (2 John 7), the denial of resurrection was utterly destructive of the purpose of the incarnation and even implied a denial of it. Paul, in a recitation of airtight theological logic, wrote, "If there is no resurrection of the dead . . . we are found false witnesses of God, because we have testified of God that He raised up Christ, whom He did not raise up—if in fact the dead do not rise. For if the dead do not rise, then Christ is not risen. And if Christ is not risen, your faith is futile; you are still in your sins!" (1 Cor. 15:13–17).

The resurrection from the dead, therefore, gives verification that death has been defeated and no longer rules as the necessary penalty for sin; if the penalty for sin has been removed, then the payment of death must have been fulfilled. God's statement that sin would bring death (Gen. 2:17; Rom. 5:12–19) has been shown as truthful in some way that relieves the sinner of the execution of this just and holy threat. That Jesus as a sinless man was raised from the dead— given the moral logic of this created order—would not be objectionable. But that it is pronounced a necessary event for forgiveness of sin involves this just man in a payment for transgressions not His own.

Jesus described His purpose in coming as "Son of Man" to give his life "a ransom for many" (Mark 10:45). Jesus selected the word "ransom" to define for the disciples the effect of the death He had been predicting (Mark 8:31; 9:31; 10:33–34). This death would be a ransom (*lutron*). Paul wrote that Jesus Christ "gave Himself [as] a ransom" (*antilutron*, 1 Tim. 2:6). This ransom constituted a payment in substitute for the death of the debtor. Paul used a strong word to indicate that Jesus's payment was done by Himself "in the stead of," as a substitute for, all (see Gen. 22:13 KJV). This substitutionary ransom occurred at a critical time, a moment designated within itself. The work of ransom occurred both in its nature and in accord with God's decree at a critical moment of its own. In Galatians, Paul expressed this as "in due [the fullness of] time," using the word for chronological time combined with the adjective that expresses maximum capacity (Gal. 6:9 NASB). The critical time (*kairos*) determined the fullness of chronological time (*chronos*). In accordance with both the critical nature of the event and the historical moment in which it was to occur, God sent His Son (Gal. 4:4). In Ephesians 1:10, Paul combines "fullness" with the word for critical time (*kairon*) for those things to come to pass that were effected only in light of the redemptive work of Christ.

Those who should die for their debt have been released by the purchase price of a sinless human life elevated to the necessity of infinite value by its indivisible union of life in an eternal divine person. None for whom this ransom has been paid will fail to receive its benefit. The ransom served in this critical time as a witness, or testimony, to God's faithfulness to His promise initiated in Genesis 3:15 concerning the victorious seed of the woman. Among the many places and variety of ways this is reiterated, we find that Haggai wrote that "the desire of all nations shall come" (Hag. 2:7). Malachi proclaimed that "the Sun of righteousness [shall] arise with healing in his wings" (Mal. 4:2). Elihu told Job, "If there is a messenger for him, a mediator, one among a thousand, to show man His uprightness, then He is gracious to him, and says, 'Deliver him from going down to the Pit; I have found a ransom'" (Job 33:23–24). David reveled in the wisdom of God that finds a way of forgiveness: "Bless the LORD, O my soul, and forget not all his benefits, who forgives all your iniquity, who heals all your diseases, who redeems your life from the pit, who crowns you with steadfast love and mercy" (Ps. 103:2–4 ESV).

This timely event of ransom qualified Jesus, the man, as the only mediator between God and man. None else could present the interest of man in an effectual way to God. Also, it opened the promises of forgiveness, the removal of transgression, to all men. The ransom covered the promise made to Abraham that "all the families" of the earth would be blessed, that he would be "father of many nations," and that "all the nations of the earth shall be blessed in him" (Gen. 12:3; 17:4–6; 18:18). Paul said, therefore, that the ransom was not for the circumcised only, not for ethnic Israel only, but for "all." The resultant message constituted Paul's call to the Gentiles as a teacher of the true faith (1 Tim. 2:5–7). The ransom for all justified his gospel ministry to Gentiles.

Paul emphasized that a free gift of justification for sinners comes through "the redemption [*apololutroseos*] that is in Christ Jesus" (Rom. 3:23–24). Paul personified redemption as a gift from God in the person of His Son, Jesus Christ, in saying that no flesh shall boast before God because it is from Him that any person is in Christ Jesus, "who became for us wisdom from God." This wisdom is seen in how Jesus Himself is made unto us "righteousness and sanctification and redemption [*apolutroseos*]" (1 Cor. 1:29–30). He Himself is the ransom price. In Ephesians, Paul wrote, "In Him we have redemption [*apolutrosin*] through His blood, the forgiveness of sins" (Eph. 1:7). The redemption is a ransom given for remission of the debt owed for sin. In verse 14 of the same chapter, Paul said that the Holy Spirit serves as a pledge of our inheritance in heaven "until the redemption [*apolutrosin*] of the purchased possession." The redemption by which we have received forgiveness and justification will come to mature fruition in a final release from the corruption of the fallen world, fallen and corruptible bodies, the partial but incomplete holiness, and the frustration of knowing in part. Again, in Colossians 1:14, Paul saw the person and work of Christ as the location ("in whom") of "redemption [*apolutrosin*] through His blood, the forgiveness of sins."

The writer of Hebrews presented Jesus as the priest who made sacrifice for the sin of the people "once for all when He offered up Himself" (Heb. 7:27). The writer then pronounced that, in the completion of the personal sacrificial offering, the Son "has been made perfect forever" (Heb. 7:28 ESV). The purpose of His incarnation reached its designed purpose in the events of sacrificial death and resurrection. The writer of Hebrews, battling against the pressure on Jewish Christians to embrace again and join in the practice of the ceremonial law, emphasized that such offerings were utterly ineffective for the thing that they so graphically symbolized. But now the antitype "has appeared once for all at the end of the ages to put away sin by the sacrifice of himself" (Heb. 9:26 ESV). This Messiah, the Christ, "having been offered once [and thus never again] to bear the sins of many, will appear a second time, not to deal with sin but to save those who are eagerly waiting for him" (9:28 ESV). Again the writer pointed to the fullness of purpose in the coming of Jesus Christ when he insisted that his readers grasp this oft–repeated truth that the sacrifices pointed to a finality and perfect fulfillment of God's will in effecting a full salvation for His people. Jesus came to do the will of the Father, and "by that will we have been sanctified through the offering of the body of Jesus Christ once for all. …For by one offering He has perfected forever those who are being sanctified…where there is remission of these [sins and lawless deeds], there is no longer an offering for sin, there is no longer any offering for sin" (10:10, 14, 18).

Hebrews discusses a better and "more excellent" covenant, a new covenant (8:6, 13). In chapter 12, the writer presented Jesus as the Mediator of a new covenant through His sprin-kled blood. This blood has brought believers from the ter-rors of the law given at Sinai (vv. 18–21)—the anticipation of certain and eternal death for those who violated it, pre-viewed even in the temporal demands surrounding its giving. This Mediator, through His sprinkled blood, superseded and put to rest the blood of Abel—the blood he gave through the sacrifice of an animal as well as the blood he shed for his faithful execution of the sacrificial requirement (v. 24). So effectual was the sprinkled blood of the Mediator of the new covenant that, instead of trembling in fear at the threats of the Mosaic covenant, those sprinkled with Jesus's blood have a radically altered prospect. To them belong all the festal glo-ries of heaven in the presence of elect angels, the redeemed of all the ages, and Jesus Himself, the Mediator of this covenant. In fact, even in the presence of God, the Judge of pure justice, does the sprinkled one find acceptance and joy (vv. 22–24). The inspired writer intended to elicit the strongest possible sense of indebtedness to the sacrifice of Christ. Fire, darkness, gloom, and a tempest of threatening wrath have given way to acceptance, assurance, and holy company in both the redeemed men and the unfallen angels. Jesus the Mediator Himself, and a smiling God, now judges us to be righteous instead of guilty.

In Hebrews 13, we learn that what is called a "new covenant" in relation to the threats of the Mosaic covenant is in reality the "everlasting covenant" (vv. 20–21). The magnitude of blessings stored in this covenant has been unleashed by the death of Christ. The "everlasting covenant" is the new covenant. It is new in the chronology of historical events and the full revelation of its provisions. But it is the covenant Paul described in 2 Timothy 1:9 in which God saves and calls us "not according to our works, but according to His own purpose and grace which was given to us in Christ Jesus before time began." We learn in Ephesians that we were chosen "in Him before the foundation of the world," which choosing for blamelessness was brought into effect by the redemptive blood of Christ (Eph. 1:4, 7).

Now this sprinkling of Christ's blood that made this "new covenant" is called "the blood of the everlasting covenant" in Hebrews 13:20. The verse defies a full understanding either in mind or heart. Consider the transcendent substance of each phrase. "Now may the God of peace"—we were His enemies but He now looks upon us as a God of peace. "Who brought up our Lord Jesus from the dead"—He put Him to death for our sins and then raised Him from the dead because any penalty for sin had been eliminated by this death. In Romans 4, Paul set this powerful and ineffable truth in these words, saying that righteousness shall be reckoned to those "who believe on the one raising our Lord Jesus Christ from the dead, who was given over to death on account of our sins and was raised on account of our justification" (Rom. 4:24–25, my translation).

We continue with the phrases of Hebrews 13:20. "That great Shepherd of the sheep"—that Shepherd who gave His life for the sheep that He might not lose one of them (John 10:11, 27–30). "In the blood of the eternal covenant"—the covenant of the grace of the Father, the redemption of the Son, and the calling and indwelling of the Holy Spirit established in the eternal counsel of the triune God for the redemption of a people. That hinge upon which the historical securing of all its provisions culminated was this shed blood of our Lord Jesus Christ.

Peter wrote that sinners were "not redeemed [*elutrothete*] with corruptible things, like silver or gold . . . but with the precious blood of Christ" (1 Peter 1:18–19). In demonstration of the kind of spirit of submission Christians should demonstrate, Peter reminded them of the submissive suffering of Christ who "bore our sins in His own body on the tree, that we, having died to sins, might live for righteousness—by whose stripes you were healed" (1 Peter 2:24). He also reminded them that "Christ also suffered once for sins, the just for the unjust, that He might bring us to God," and that this work was fully secured and attested "through the resurrection of Jesus Christ, who has gone into heaven and is at the right hand of God" (1 Peter 3:18, 21–22).

John clearly set the work of Christ in the context of His ransom in stating that "the blood of Jesus Christ His Son cleanses us from all sin" (1 John 1:7). This cleansing is effected because Jesus is "the propitiation for our sins" (2:2). The truth stands indelibly in the edict of eternity and in its execution in history that "in this is love, not that we loved God, but that He loved us and sent His Son to be the propitiation for our sins" (4:10).

It is impossible to obey the Pauline injunction to "remember Jesus Christ, risen from the dead, the offspring of David, as preached in my gospel" if we do not embrace with heart, mind, and strength the substitutionary death of Christ for sinners. A conscience that can go before the righteous Judge of heaven and earth without a plea that one who is worthy has borne his punishment and granted him righteousness has not dealt with the gospel in repentance and faith. The substitutionary death of Christ, a wrath–receiving sacrifice who gave up Himself voluntarily to this end, is not a theory of the atonement or a perspective among others but the very teaching of Christ Himself and the passionate faith as well as the revealed truth communicated through His apostles. If we do not claim this as our only hope before a righteous God, then we do not possess the hope of eternal life.

15

Remember Jesus Christ Even When the World Says to Forget Him

One of the great ironies of Liberalism is this: They thought they were recovering an authentic historical Jesus while they dismembered the Jesus of the New Testament and historic orthodoxy. That the incarnation brought into the world eternal God in human flesh, that the purpose of this incarnation was to effect forgiveness of sins and a perfect righteousness granting the reality of eternal life for those who will repent of sin and trust in Jesus because of His salvific work, and that this person and this way of salvation is revealed to us in a coherent, progressive, non–contradictory revelation now gathered into a single book called the Bible—all were absurd and demonstrably false propositions, so they taught. While they thought that they were indeed remembering Jesus, or recovering Him from layers of irrational, non–historical authoritarianism, despotism, and mystical–oriented individualism, they deconstructed Him and taught the world to forget Him. Their Jesus is not the one Paul told us to remember. Liberalism most clearly pays little if any attention to Paul's concern that this be "in accordance with my gospel."

According to Shailer Mathews (1863–1941), "those of us who have been compelled by study and experience to distinguish between the values perpetuated in the Christian religion and the formulas and practices in which they have been expressed, believe that we are neither obstinate nor hypocritical in our endeavor to relieve the Christian from the burden of outgrown patterns of thought and enforced loyalty to that which hinders religious faith."[48] Mathews and others interpreted their destructive and reckless endeavor as a rescue mission.

In *The Faith of Modernism* (1925), Mathews sought to demonstrate the irrelevance and narrowness of historically orthodox Christianity. He ridiculed inerrancy, substitutionary atonement, the doctrine of eternal punishment, and orthodox Christology as irrelevant to the needs of the modern world. Christianity is not doctrinaire, he claimed, focusing on theological formulas and structures of religious authority; it is, rather, a living and ongoing experience of the way that Jesus viewed God and met the needs of man. Christianity is not about truth but love.[49]

Mathews defended Modernism as "concerned with the historical method of discovering the permanent values of Christianity, and the religious rather than the theological test of religion." It is not interested so much in theology as in life. It seeks to discover and restate for modernity the "permanent significance of evangelical Christianity to human life."[50] He said in another place, "The simple fact is that the center of interest in religion is passing from theology to life."[51] Historic orthodoxy, Mathews contended, is "interested in theological regularity" while Modernism places its emphasis on "religious development and scientific method."[52] Modernism sees Christianity as a religion whose moral standards, views of God, and doctrinal development have evolved within the framework of history. Theology depends much more on frame of mind within historical eras than upon any supposed static truth contained in a book of revealed propositions. Even the Bible is a record of the religious perceptions of a variety of types of people. Some views are helpful according to modern standards and some indefensible. It is within the "life" of developing humanity that views of God grow to be accepted or rejected according to scientific knowledge and critical historical understanding.

What are the implications of separating theology from life? Supposedly, the "life" that is Christianity abides irrespective of any consideration of truth and flows from a perception of the spirit and confident Sonship manifest by Christ. His spirit and internalization of the purpose and character of God abides unchangeably, unperturbable by the shifting categories of theology or views of biblical truthfulness.

William Newton Clarke (1842–1911) stated his ideal of "life" as opposed to theology, even "life" as opposed to Scripture, in unmistakable terms. "But I think it must be God's will," Clarke pontificated, "that the time shall come when the means gives way to the end; when *confidence in the living God himself stands independent of any views that we may hold of the book in which we have read most about him.*"[53] Because biblical criticism has made and continues to make such substantial changes in the credibility of its historical and doctrinal narratives, "all Christians need a faith in God that no changes in knowledge of the Bible can disturb."[54] So faith in God, ostensibly Christian faith in God, must be maintained apart from any grasp of doctrinal truth communicated through the book that claims to be "God breathed." Of course! Clarke and Mathews, and all liberals along with them, would chime in, "I am sure that God intends such a faith for us all." The faith that depends upon any confidence in a written "thus saith the Lord" is an occasion for remorse for "it is a sorrow to find a certain type of belief in the Bible standing in the way of such faith in God himself."[55]

In his systematic theology, *An Outline of Christian Theology,* Clarke said, "The Christian revelation was not made in a book, or in writing, or by dictation, but in life and action, especially by the living Christ."[56] Clarke virtually made a theological career out of distinguishing between the living influence of Christ and the inerrancy of Scripture. "Perfect accuracy of statement, or what is now named inerrancy, was not sought in the composition of the Scripture," Clarke wrote. Further he expressed, "Nor can we see why the divine

Spirit should lodge inerrancy in a single manuscript, to be lost as soon as copies of it were multiplied."[57] He stated his commitment to a final contradiction between inerrancy and the vital flow of Christian life in a statement that said the latter eliminates the possibility of the former:

> The free and natural method of the Bible has opened actual experience to our sight and given us the divine realities in human life in all their freshness and power; and this quality of livingness is worth more to us than what we call inerrancy would be. We could not have both, for an influence sufficient to make inerrancy would have put an end to the simple human experience of God's presence and taken away the naturalness of the Scriptures.[58]

Walter Rauschenbusch (1861–1918) pressed the idea of the priority and authority of human consciousness with relentless consistency. He viewed the Bible as a witness to developing *human experience* of God and *consciousness* of God seen and felt most clearly by Jesus. The Jesus he wanted was the Jesus who initiated the kingdom of God as described through the social experience and conscience of Rauschenbusch. Nothing else in Scripture could be seen as valid content for doing theology. Everything except his perception of democratic social conscience should be relegated to a category of curiously immature, or even destructive, views of God. In looking through Scripture, Rauschenbusch selected as relevant "those theoretical ideas which agree with our experience, and are cold to those which have never entered into our life." He called this experiential authority "a kind of theological referendum, a democratic change in theology on the basis of religious experience."[59]

Mathews, continuing his anti–Bible recitation in full approval of Clarke's bookless faith of the future, informed his readers that "facts appear which make belief in its verbal inerrancy untenable."[60] In an amazingly simplistic caricature of believers in verbal inspiration, Mathews wrote, "If the Bible is to be taken as verbally inerrant, then we must hold that God has hands large enough to cover the cleft in the rock in which a prophet hides. Not to take it literally is to abandon the principle of inerrancy formulated as a doctrine."[61] The Modernist rather than the inerrantist is the true successor of the great biblical interpreters of the past, for he knows "how to separate between the permanent and the temporary in its pages."[62] In consequence, Mathews's Modernist can enjoy "the spiritual ministry of the Bible." He cares not for any disturbance to its claims by radical historicist criticism "which the believer in the inerrancy of the scriptures has either to answer or to denounce."[63]

Mathews explained this Bibleless Christianity more fully. Carefree criticism does not touch the spirit of the Modernist Christian—he has no vested interest in the Bible, after all— for "the historical and critical study of the scriptures does not begin with a doctrine of inspiration," at least not the kind that must be transferred to the biblical text. "Modernists believe in inspiration," Mathews averred, "rather than inerrancy," because this inspiration does not extend to the words of Scripture but is "the inspiration of men, not of words."[64] In this way he could press to its full extent the idea that spiritual life preceded the written text. The Bible "sprang from our religion, not our religion from the Bible."[65] The Bible is a "trustworthy record of human experiences of God," Mathews explained.[66] The reader must either laugh or be completely baffled by the use of "trustworthy" in this doctrinal disaster. "For what?" we must ask. Mathews continued that this record of experiences demonstrated "the growing understanding of God" in establishing attitudes and convictions that found fullest and effective expression in Jesus Christ and inspired the religious group He founded.[67] Those attitudes and convictions may develop in each generation and can be more influential in our own lives and in our modern world.

Harry Emerson Fosdick (1878–1969) was known nationwide through his radio broadcast as the Counselor of America. He was a student of William Newton Clarke and the pastor of John D. Rockefeller and James Colgate. Fosdick described the critical event that led him to reject biblical inerrancy. He recounted reading a title by Andrew D. White, *History of the Warfare of Science with Theology in Christendom.* To him it seemed unanswerable. The facts on this issue concerning "the assumed infallibility of the Scriptures" were distressing to him and had the power of an undeniable oracle. A commitment to infallibility "had impeded research, deepened and prolonged obscurantism, fed the mania of persecution, and held up the progress of mankind." Fosdick declared, "I no longer believed the old stuff I had been taught. Moreover, I no longer merely doubted it. I rose in indignant revolt against it."[68]

Certainly, in the view of Shailer Mathews and other Modernists, an inerrant Bible "hinders religious faith." If Paul's definitive statement, "according to my gospel," implies the revelatory foundation of apostolic teaching (and it does), then to reject biblical infallibility is to forget Jesus Christ. William Newton Clarke gave a decade–by–decade description of his journey from fundamentalist confidence in Scripture to his liberation of soul and mind from the intellectual prison of inerrancy. He discovered that he was not obliged to "agree with these writers in all that they had written." Certainly, he had no duty to "look upon them as infallible guides" or "to accept all statements in the Bible as true and all views it contained as correct." He was led to this position by "examination of the book itself. Its own contents bore witness to its errancy." He "dated this conviction against the inerrancy of the Bible" as occurring in the 1870s.[69]

In Clarke's journey toward being the first fully committed liberal systematic theologian among the Baptists, he gloried in his breakthrough to a confidence in his intrinsic ability to discern the useful from the unuseful, the congenial from the uncongenial, in biblical propositions. "According to the principle that I accepted and acted upon," Clarke explained, "a system of Christian theology has God for its center, the spirit of Jesus for its organizing principle, and *congenial truth from the Bible* and *from without* for its material." He scoffed at the idea that all the Bible was profitable for doctrine; in fact, he thought a good bit of it is unprofitable. Some sections *are not congenial to the spirit of Jesus* which dominates Christian theology, and some express truth in forms that cannot be of permanent validity." Rather, the theologian has to discern within the Bible's content those parts and genres that instruct him "in that spirit of Christ which is the organizing principle" and that provide him "with abundant congenial material for the building up of doctrine."[70]

The method that treats all of Scripture as profitable for doctrine—that is, those who believe in plenary verbal inspiration—"stands historically upon the foundation of an equal and infallible inspiration." These theologians work as if "the eternal Spirit gave to these writers truth and thought and words, and thus imparted his own infallibility and authority to what they wrote." But, according to Clarke, the more we know about the Bible from critical study, "the less does it match the theory of an inspiration that imparts infallibility to all its statements." Narrow and uninformed people affirm that Christianity "stands or falls with infallible inspiration." In this way, Clarke asserted, "theology is burdened with a task that cannot be performed."[71]

The Modernists completely abolished the historical teachings of Christianity, for they ingeniously re-engineered the place of the Bible in defining it. If one successfully makes the Bible only a witness to experience, which witness is progressive and correctable, then contemporary experience becomes just as relevant for defining Christianity as ancient experience. We all can attain to the same confidence in God as Father based on the principle of love that Jesus had. In so doing, we become sons of God like Him.

The redefinition of Christianity attempted by liberals could not proceed, much less succeed, if an authoritative revelation concerning creation, Christ, crucifixion, and consummation existed. They had to rid the world of any authoritative revelation, especially one deemed to be infallible as breathed out by God and, therefore, inerrant in its resulting text. Paul's admonition, "according to my gospel," necessitates a commitment to the entirety of the witness of the Old Testament and the witness to the life and teachings of Jesus (all of them) collected and set forth with literary purpose by the apostolic community. The Liberals really did want the church to forget Jesus Christ, not remember Him.

16

Remember Jesus Christ in the Midst of Liberal Criticism

Friedrich Schleiermacher (1768–1834) set the stage for the Liberal[72] disremembrance of Christ. In his unnerving wrestling with the question as to how Jesus is the redeemer and how He sets the standard for what it means to be Christian, Schleiermacher had to deal with what he called the "pure historicity of the person of the Redeemer."[73] By historicity, the father of Liberal theology did not mean that all the Bible reports of Jesus is historically true, but that Jesus had to be subject to the kinds of historical development and influences of all humans. He expanded the idea a bit in writing that "whatever is involved in the ideality of the contents of His personal spiritual life must also be compatible with this purely human conception of his historical existence."[74] The person of Christ, summarily, he defined in terms of a human with a heightened God–consciousness: "The Redeemer, then, is like all men in virtue of the identity of human nature, but distinguished from them all by the constant potency of His God–consciousness, which was a veritable existence of God in Him."[75] Pervasive within Liberal thought is this focus on the God–consciousness of Jesus as that which drives us to assert His divinity and makes it legitimate to call the religion He initiated "Christianity."

David Strauss (1808–1874), in his pursuit of the mythological nature of the biblical record of Jesus's life, stressed the impossibility of the virgin birth as well as its incompatibility with the nature of the New Testament literature. Not only must we consent to the "exceptionless experience that only by the concurrence of the two sexes is a new human being generated," but we must also accept his literary judgment to "abide by the mythical interpretation of our narrative." The reader must be content "with gathering from it no particular fact in the life of Jesus, but only a new proof how strong was the impression of his messiahship left by Jesus on the minds of his contemporaries." Even the birth narratives supposedly employ this purposely crafted mythology in a messianic form.[76]

William Newton Clarke tipped the hand of American and Baptist Modernism expressed in theological Liberalism toward the theological reductionism of Adolf von Harnack (1851–1930). Clarke contended that the first alien and corrupting influence on "the Christian doctrine" was Greek philosophy. All one need do is contrast "the Sermon on the Mount and the Nicene Creed."[77] He saw the contrast as "both sharp and deep." The Creed of Nicea, so assumed

Clarke, "added to the bulk of doctrine, but not to its vitality."[78] Though Clarke was the closest to historic orthodoxy of the Modernist methodologists, he joined the whole group in minimizing the importance of the creedal developments of the first five centuries. Pushing into the background the importance of accurate doctrinal definitions he highlighted an emphasis on Christianity's distillation into a certain kind of attitude rather than affirming the necessity of a certain content of belief.

In *An Outline of Christian Theology*, seeking to focus on a singular kind of consciousness that was in Jesus, Clarke rejected out of hand the possibility of Jesus's simultaneous consciousness of His eternal Sonship and His identity with humanity. Clarke emphasized that Jesus was "a genuine person, possessed of a consciousness and a will," but "not two consciousnesses and two wills." Contemplating the inference from orthodoxy that Jesus was one person "possessed of two consciousnesses and wills, a divine and a human," Clarke doubted that such a being could be called a "person." He recognized that "many believers in the Incarnation have supposed that Jesus carried through life a double consciousness, acting sometimes from one and sometimes from the other." Strangely ignoring the biblical facts—such as hunger on the one hand and multiplication of bread and fish on the other—that prompt such a judgment, Clarke contended that this observation was "contrary to the record." If Jesus were a person, as the concept of incarnation suggests that He certainly was, He like other persons had "a single consciousness and a single will" and consequently was "capable of living a genuine personal life." Clarke strongly resisted "*a priori* assumptions as to what an incarnation must accomplish, even if they were much better grounded than this one." Should we ask if this single consciousness were divine or human, "the answer is that strictly it was neither. It was unique, partaking of both qualities, human and divine."[79] Later, in a discussion of the atonement, Clarke seems to capitulate to the "man in perfect accord with the divine will" understanding of how Jesus presents God to us. "Christ was in humanity, a man, and yet with God so expressed in him that he was truly divine."[80]

Not only does Clarke's Christology confuse the believer as to whether Jesus as one person had both a human nature (with all relevant constituent elements) and a divine nature—that is, the fleshly embodiment of the eternal Son of God so that the holy being conceived in Mary would legitimately be called the Son of God (Luke 1:35)—but he would bid us believe that even Jesus could not obey the Pauline admonition to "remember Jesus Christ." His consciousness, according to Clarke, was neither human nor divine. Did Jesus know who He was?

Though Clarke is the most traditional of the Liberals, he minimized the importance of theological formulation by his emphasis on the life and spirit of Christianity. These coordinate aspects of consciousness he wielded as a weapon against synthesis of biblical propositions into systematic truth. The Council of Nicea (325), the Council of Chalcedon (451), and the *Tome* of Leo (449), according to Clarke, had little substantial relevance to the real issue of Christian doctrine.

"But do not fail to notice how the Christian doctrine came into existence," he chastened. "Do not imagine that it came by being formulated some fine day by the decree of some great council, or by the command or endorsement of authorized men." No, it was built on the popular perception of the fitness of certain biblical ideas—but not all—that witnessed to the popular conscience. "The teaching of Jesus did not grow into doctrine by being discussed and officially interpreted."[81]

Present Christian discernment allows us to ignore some things that the apostles "said or wrote" so that those words and ideas need not enter "into the substance of the Christian doctrine." So it is with the words of Jesus; not all are of equal value and not all need enter into our grasp of what it means to be Christian. Doctrine as presently conceived and as ministering to the concerns of modern people had no careful crafters who sought to fit together biblical material into consistent doctrines within a consistent framework. "Doctrine was no such formal, external thing as to take up something merely because it had been said," Clarke asserted in a spirit of omniscience, "even though it were by the Lord himself." So strange and dangerous it is that he takes the Petrine reprimand of Jesus into his own theological method—"Not so, Lord" (Matt. 16:22). Instead, Christian doctrine "grew as a vital thing, and grew in the soil of life. The Christian doctrine sprang up in the experience of Christian living. It was the Christian truth as learned by the Christian people." If a thought, no matter how well attested within the Bible, "did not take root in this vital soil, and take root to stay and live," it did not become a part of the Christian doctrine. "The process was simply a vital process of assimilation."[82] One may clearly see that the Liberals introduced, through science and historicism, a new standard of what constituted things necessary for life. In this redefinition, they severely pared what could survive as the "vital soil" of Christian belief.

Rauschenbusch made no pretensions to hide his strong rejection of infallibility or even the distinct inspiration of the apostles. "Those who have first–hand experience of inspiration either in their own souls or in the life of others, have always combined reverence for the authority of the word of the Lord and a realization of the human frailty and liability to error in the prophet." Since inspiration all the way from the prophets to the apostles to the church since the New Testament has been an ongoing occurrence, we may be assured that "inspiration did not involve infallibility when men knew it by experience."[83] The leveling of inspiration through the ages allowed Rauschenbusch to point to teachings of "inspired" men whose ideas had been outdated to seal his point. "There are many degrees of clarity and power in this living inspiration," Rauschenbusch explained, "and heavy admixtures of human error, passion, and false sentiment."[84] Whereas the old view of an infallible inspiration resulting in an inerrant and finally authoritative text was necessary "to keep doctrine undisturbed," the changing conditions of society and culture called for new prophets who would utter inspired messages and effective strategies to present "some sense of antagonism between the will of God and the present order of things."[85]

Rauschenbusch also joined in the celebration of Harnack's

severe reductionistic method of analyzing the biblical text and the doctrinal development of Christian thought according to the materialistic assumptions of contemporary science and the immovable historicist methods of dealing with texts. "We shall not get away again from the central proposition of Harnack's History of Dogma," Rauschenbusch affirmed with greater devotion to Harnack than to the biblical text, "that the development of Catholic dogma was the process of the Hellenization of Christianity." According to the Harnackian naturalistic worldview, "alien influences streamed into the religion of Jesus Christ and created a theology which he never taught nor intended. What would Jesus have said to the symbol of Chalcedon or the Athanasian Creed if they had been read to him?"[86] Distinguishing between Jesus as God in the flesh and Jesus as a religious personality was a major theme of Liberals. Again, we turn to Rauschenbusch, who asserted, "So we have in Jesus a perfect religious personality, a spiritual life completely filled by the realization of a God who is love."[87]

Shailer Mathews sought to sing lead in the chorus of those who pit religion against truth, saying, "But if Christianity is a religion, it cannot be treated as if it were a group of absolute truths."[88] Mathews explained how receiving Jesus as a religious person leads to significant modification of biblical propositions and historic orthodoxy.

> The substitution of Jesus for authoritative doctrines, the conception of Christianity as a movement which undertakes to reproduce his attitudes and consequent

> behavior in our own day, the softening of God's sovereignty into a divine paternity, the development of the social gospel and the substitution of Christian nurture for supernatural conversion of children suffering from a corrupt human nature inherited from Adam, the modification of doctrines of the atonement were the direct result of the substitution of scientific attitude for that of implicit reliance on the Bible, demanded by orthodoxy.[89]

To the Liberal mind, historic orthodoxy may or may not be true; it is immaterial to the central core of Christianity. In fact, "If Christianity is intrinsically a system of doctrines authoritatively fixed in patterns of other times and lacking moral content, it will be abandoned."[90] The irony is obvious: The Liberals made their required cultural adjustment and, in the process, abandoned Christianity.

Jesus's divinity was not a matter of essence but of personal accomplishment. His determination of will and compliance of spirit, His unrelenting efforts to know God and communicate His spirit of love and acceptance constituted His goodness. Shailer Mathews, who cautiously used the nomenclature of "deity," defined it once as "the revealed presence of God to be met in his life."[91] In a slight expansion of his definition of Jesus's deity, he pointed to "the religious appeal of Jesus himself, his power to evoke religious faith."[92] Christian faith centers in "god in a man, not in a man made into a God." Jesus was "empowered by God's resident spirit to accomplish . . . deliverance." Jesus was "the giver of God to men, the revealer of God's way of saving men."[93]

Pauline thought introduced certain ideas of preexistence borrowed from the culture, in Mathews's discussion, but did not alter the fundamental idea that in Jesus men's "religious needs found satisfaction."[94] All theories of atonement only point to this basic primitive conviction that Jesus is the person "through whom God revealed salvation." That through centuries men have had their religious needs met in their loyalty to Jesus "argues the sanity of their conviction that God was in him," that "real God has been met when men trust a real Jesus as His revealer."[95]

The councils of the fourth and fifth centuries are completely understandable in light of the Christian attempt to "account for this unique power of Jesus to minister like God to their religious needs," under the influence of the "Hellenization" of Christianity. Their ideas of "substance" and their metaphysical discussions are all outmoded and irrelevant for Modernists, but did, nevertheless, express "a permanent conviction as to the saving revelation of God through Jesus Christ." If, however, such creedal formulas were taken as expressing necessary truths to be believed, this "would exclude the apostles if not Jesus himself from the Christian religion."[96]

Based on his literary analysis of the gospels and his resistance to any biblical assertion that seemed to challenge the present state of scientific inquiry, not only did Mathews consider the virgin birth an indelicate discussion, but he said that "our knowledge of biological facts makes a human virgin birth as difficult of belief as our knowledge of astronomy makes it impossible for us to think that day and night existed before the sun was created."[97] So, given the highly compromised text and worldview of the Scripture writers and the overly zealous propensity for theological consistency of some church fathers, what can one say about Paul's admonition to "remember Jesus Christ"? Mathews answered, "In him we feel that we can see as much of God and of His character as is possible for an individual to express. . . . This experience has been too many million time[s] repeated to be denied."[98] We do not, therefore, focus in any saving way on the person and work of Christ Himself but seek as much as we can, in light of the limited and consistently mutable character of our knowledge, to express in our consciousness the same humanly limited consciousness of God's love and Fatherhood that Jesus had.

Rauschenbusch complained that theologians such as Athanasius who wrote epochal discussions of Jesus as they perceived him "give no indication that the personality of Jesus was live and real to them." Not essence but effort constituted Jesus's manifestation of divinity. "In all other cases we judge the ethical worth of a man by the character he achieves by will and effort," Rauschenbusch insisted. "If he has any unusual outfit of nature we deduct it in our estimate." In that light, he asked, "How can we claim high ethical value for the personality and character of Jesus if no effort of will was necessary to achieve it?" Instead of having brought with Him an intrinsic impeccability, "the divine quality of his personality" emerges from the "free and ethical acts of his will" rather than "the passive inheritance of a divine essence."[99] We should find a determined and struggling "only human" Jesus more attractive and assuring than the Jesus who was "begotten, not made, who came down and was made flesh and was made man" (325 Nicene Creed).

The Liberals worked with all the tools at their disposal to make sure they were clear in concluding that Jesus is not God. If He were God, so they reason, we should exalt Him less for what He thought and taught than if He were a man, having no gifts or nature above ours. The Christianity of Liberalism did not want a Jesus we can worship but a Jesus whose accomplishments as a man defy the orthodox assumptions of human nature. We are "Christians" because Jesus shows us the true potential of our nature; He shows us how the principle of love operates; He teaches us to see God as Father in the same way He experienced God as Father and knew His own Sonship in a way that we too can know it. He exhibits such God consciousness that He leads us all to the same perception of God's benevolent presence in all lives. At the same time (again we are called upon to embrace the irony as endemic to the theological task), we are free to minimize the importance and truthfulness of some of the things that the gospel writers reported Him to have said.

The assumption is that Jesus surely was just a man, born of Mary and of Joseph but purely attuned to the character and will of God and given over totally to the triumph of the kingdom of God on earth. As Rauschenbusch articulated with a destructive piety, "We shall come closer to the secret of Jesus if we think less of the physical process of conception and more of the spiritual processes of desire, choice, affirmation, and self–surrender within his own will and personality."[100] This argument suggests that perplexities about many of the events and propositions of Scripture simply do not deserve the time historically spent on them. Through critical studies, we are able to discern the fabulous, mythical, age–centric, immature and otherwise unworthy elements in the biblical text and sift out the pure. We can discern the experience, and thus the mind, of Christ in the midst of what is unworthy of Him. "The mind of Jesus is our criterion for an ethical scrutiny" of any supposed doctrine presented to us in Scripture.[101]

Rauschenbusch found in Johann Gottlieb Fichte (1762–1814), the German idealistic philosopher, an articulate spokesman for Jesus's personal God–consciousness as the sum of His divinity and saviorhood. Fichte opined that "the consciousness of the absolute unity of the human and the divine life is the profoundest insight possible to man." None before Jesus had this insight, and, therefore, "it is really true that Jesus of Nazareth, in a unique way, true of no other, is the only begotten and first born Son of God." Because He was the first, and perhaps still the most profound, "it remains incontestably true that all those who since Jesus have arrived at union with God, have attained it only through him and by his mediation."[102]

The brilliance of the natural intelligence and the circuitous plausibility of Modernist reasoning staggers credibility when one realizes that they so constructed their arguments as to convince themselves that their goal was noble and redemptive. While they everywhere implied, and often stated explicitly, that historic Christianity served to hide Christ, they argued so subtly and with such elaborate turns of phrase, using beautiful words without substance, that they generated great zeal and determination to use Christ as their main weapon against Christianity. Such arrogant confidence is almost impossible to fathom; in opposition, not only to the two millennia of Christian witness, but also to the Bible and the apostolic preaching itself, they constructed a Christianity from modern intellectual assumptions and proclaimed their obliteration of Christian truth as the triumph of the permanent in Christianity.[103]

To our theme, therefore, we return. As on the authority of Scripture, so on the person of Christ the Liberals engaged in a conspiracy to make Paul's apostolic admonition irrelevant. "Remember Jesus Christ, risen from the dead, the offspring of David, as preached in my gospel" (2 Tim. 2:8 ESV). Such serious calls to doctrinal fidelity had little conscience–driven importance to the Liberal disapprovers of biblically derived, historic, creedally confessional orthodoxy. Their comments on Paul's sense of authority would amount to scoffing.

17

Remember the Cross of Jesus Christ

COUNTERING LIBERAL REJECTION OF
PENAL SUBSTITUTIONARY ATONEMENT

When Satan told Eve, "You will not surely die," (Gen. 3:4), he convinced her that God's threat that sin deserved death would be submissive to His mercy. God would forgive, or perhaps merely overlook, sin without inflicting the ultimate penalty. Liberal views of the atonement show a sense of revulsion toward the concept that sin deserves wrath and will not be set aside apart from a just resolution of the threat of death and the actual disobedience. The God who revealed Himself as "forgiving iniquity and transgression and sin," while at the same time "by no means clearing the guilty" (Ex. 34:7), was unknown to them. This supposed revelation was a mere psycho/cultural dream of Moses.

William Newton Clarke wrote the commentary on Mark in the *American Commentary* (1881). In dealing with Jesus's words on the cross, "My God, My God, why have You forsaken Me?" (Mark 15:34), he distanced himself as far as possible from any idea of penal substitution and the display of divine wrath. Though agonizing as the cry is and difficult the interpretation, Clarke was utterly certain that it did not involve any kind of abandonment or anger of the Father in relation to Jesus. "It was not extorted from our Saviour by an actual desertion on the part of his Father, a changing of his Father's feeling toward him from love and approval to wrath."[104] Because Jesus was doing the Father's will, and did only those things that pleased the Father, it was impossible that He experienced in His soul and on His body an actual display of wrath. In the supreme moment of His obedience, it is "morally impossible" that "God turned away from him in wrath." The idea that God "supposed him to be guilty and was therefore angry at him" is just as impossible, for God never supposes what is not true and never punishes the innocent as if they were guilty. Thus, Clarke pushed away the idea of imputation as operative in Christ's sense of abandonment. The suffering of Jesus "was not, strictly, penal suffering."[105] Though Clarke left that moment in the realm of impenetrable mystery, he attempted an explanation. Jesus's deep consciousness of "unity with God was overpowered by his sense of his unity with sinful men." Though He shared the Father's revulsion against sin, His overwhelming experience of its nature as hostile to goodness and righteousness shut off His consciousness of unity with God. "Thus his unity with God brought him no relief," Clarke theorized, "but only intensified his woe and helped to take away the sense of its own preciousness." In that moment of dereliction, "the sense of his unity with men overpowered the sense of his unity with God and brought the whole burden of the world's sin upon his consciousness of the helpful presence of his Father." Clarke believes that the mental energy exerted in seeking to show the connection of this moment with redemption has minimized necessary attention to "the significance of the cross by way of example."[106]

Clarke reiterated the same idea more than a decade later in his book *An Outline of Christian Theology*: "Now, upon the cross, he felt his unity with the sinful race so profoundly as to lose his sense of unity with God his Father, and cried out in the agony of desolation, 'My God, my God, why hast thou forsaken me?'"[107] The entire sense of abandonment and divine displeasure was an act of Jesus's consciousness, not an objective reality. Clarke began this discussion with the question, "What view of the work of Christ is to be presented here?" Immediately he answered, "Not any one of the great historic theories." He rejected the concept of ransom and also "that Christ paid to God a satisfaction equivalent to the sins that God was to forgive."[108] All theories of substitution, penal satisfaction, propitiation as a manifestation of divine wrath, and even moral government theories were rejected by Clarke. That Christ was punished for sins that God would forgive could not be justified in Clarke's system of thought.

In fact, if the cross involved a punishment for sin in any sense, forgiveness could not be seen as a distinct mercy of God, for "the same sin cannot be both punished and forgiven."[109] Since forgiveness implies the foregoing of punishment and restoration to fellowship, that sin was imputed to Christ would not express the gospel but be a contradiction of it. "Punishment is absolutely untransferable," Clarke reiterated, "and no one can possibly be punished for the sin of another."[110] If imputation of sin to Christ cannot take place, neither can another's righteousness be assumed or supposed as the possession of an unrighteousness person. Clarke asserted, "There is no unreal changing of places, or imputation to any one of character that does not belong to him."[111] So the cross manifests both satisfaction and propitiation in that it gives satisfaction to God that He has given an ultimate demonstration of His desire to draw men to salvation in the unjust infliction of sin's perverse cruelty on the righteous Christ. The propitiation was not done and finished by Christ's death but only revealed the eternal fatherly attitude of grace toward sinners who will lament their evil and turn to righteousness. "Through the life and death of Christ," Clarke wrote, "God has given expression, for his own satisfaction as well as for the sake of winning men, to the truth that by voluntary and perpetual sin–bearing he is doing all that his own demand requires for the saving of sinful men." God is perpetually doing what was done in Christ's death, and it is "thus that when Christ is called a propitiation he is said to have been made such by the act of God. God's own sin–bearing satisfied God, and his exhibition of it in Christ completes his satisfaction."[112]

Clarke further concluded that reconciliation does not come from a moral transaction but is an abiding desire and constant openness of God to receive returning sinners. God is willing for reconciliation to take place, but men are not willing. The life of Christ and His willingness to suffer the consequences of human sin demonstrated "the spirit in which God endures that he may save."[113] According to Clarke, when Jesus bore the cruelty of those who tried and crucified Him, He was bearing human sin in His own body as a manifestation of God's willingness to endure, perhaps even tolerate, and be patient with the solidarity of human sin, to urge men to "be reconciled to God." "Suffering borne for salvation's sake is at once heart–breaking and winning to the one for whom it is endured."[114] It has no objective effectuality in itself but is the highest indication of the patience and beckoning of God to sinners of His willingness to restore them to wholeness of life here and in eternity to "the higher stages of that divine life which has already begun."[115]

Clarke's view of the cross, reduced to its most basic assertion, is the "Moral Influence Theory of the work of Christ." Though some think it to be inadequate, Clarke observed, none "can fail to cherish the truth that it contains." That Christ was willing to bear such suffering at the hands of sinful men to woo them to part with sin and seek righteousness, "who can resist the drawing of such love and righteousness as we here behold?"[116]

Walter Rauschenbusch shared Clarke's resistance to the biblical concepts of the atonement as expressed in its orthodox and Protestant confessional development; he did it with more determination and certainty. While Clarke used phrases like "the best human thought, springing from the best experience, . . . the present tendency of Christian thought,

...Christian thought in our time,"[117] Rauschenbusch boldly stated the superior interpretive capacities of his generation to any of the past. Historicism runs rampant in Rauschenbusch's *A Theology for the Social Gospel.* All religions, and doctrines in those religions, have their origin in the historical manifestation of human experience. Virtually all development is immanent, not based on any truly comprehended, unchanging, transcendent truth, certainly not on revelation under the assumption of infallibility. The perceived challenge of the day provides the intellectual energy for formulation of principial answers. "Our dominant ideas," Rauschenbusch said in exaltation of Modernist methodology, "are personality and social solidarity." So we must ask, "Has the death of Christ any relation to these?"[118]

Continuing the spirit of the triumph of modern systems of criticism, historicism, and social theory, Rauschenbusch issued his assertion of the interpretive prerogative of cultural relativism over all fields of human endeavor, including theology: "Have we not just as much right to connect this supreme religious event with our problems as Paul and Anselm and Calvin, and to use the terminology and methods of our day?" The question was rhetorical and assertive. He left no doubt concerning his answer. "In so far as the historical and social sciences have taught our generation to comprehend solidaristic facts, we are in a better situation to understand the atonement than any previous generation,"[119] obviously including the first–century apostles. He would have none of Paul's confident admonition contained in his qualifying statement, "according to my gospel."

After a brief discussion of the views of Anselm, Lutherans, and Calvinists, Rauschenbusch instructed, "These traditional theological explanations of the death of Christ have less biblical authority than we are accustomed to suppose." Then he listed those he found unsuitable. "The fundamental terms and ideas—'satisfaction,' 'substitution,' 'imputation,' merit'—are post–biblical ideas, and are alien from the spirit of the gospel." When Jesus died for our sins, did He do it by imputation? No. "Both guilt and merit are personal" and neither "can be transferred from one person to another."[120] Attempts to explain atonement "on the basis of law and in forensic terms . . . shock our Christian feeling" and "wipe out the love and mercy of God, our most essential Christian conviction."[121]

As is true in virtually every liberal discussion of salvation, the concept of individualism is seen as a true distraction from proper understanding (except in some aspects of Fosdick's construction). Theology of the past trained people to think in terms of their personal salvation, personal forgiveness, and personal justification. The exhibiting of repentance and faith were for the personal, individual benefits of present justification and in the future eternal life. "How did Jesus bear our sins?" Rauschenbusch asked. We have not answered this fittingly because "the bar to a true understanding of the atonement has been our individualism." Jesus did not "in any sense bear the sin of some ancient Briton who beat up his wife in B. C. 56, or of some mountaineer in Tennessee who got drunk in A. D. 1917." He bore the weight of the "public sins of organized society."[122]

Rauschenbusch identified six of these public sins, the cumulative effect of which was to lash out against the purity of Jesus and His speckless perception of God's way of dealing with human evil. Jesus's death came from the consolidation of these six deadly social sins identified by Rauschenbusch as religious bigotry, graft and political power, corruption of justice, mob spirit and mob action, militarism, and class contempt. He bore the sin of the world in that His life and teaching contradicted the prevailing oppressive powers of society and, refusing to endorse the "Kingdom of Evil," they snatched His life from Him. Pressing down on his resistance to punitive elements, or imputation, the social gospel champion again argued, "Jesus bore these sins in no legal or artificial sense, but in their impact on his own body and soul."[123]

"It is not a legal theory of imputation," Rauschenbusch reiterated, "but a conception of spiritual solidarity, by which our own free and personal acts constitute us partakers of the guilt of others."[124] It was an intensification of the life experience of Jesus, "an integral part of his life." Earlier theorists about Jesus's death "made a fundamental mistake in treating the atonement as something distinct, and making the life of Jesus a mere stage for his death, a matter almost negligible in the work of salvation."[125] The effectiveness of the atonement has nothing to do with the amount of suffering nor the supposed satisfaction to the wrath of an offended deity. His death had the "same significance" as the consistent course of His life, a life of uncompromised service and love manifesting itself in the "highest and hardest part of his life work."[126] He took His place rejoicingly with the prophets who were so persecuted.[127] His death showed the power of sin in humanity, constituted the supreme manifestation of love, and reinforced prophetic religion in opposition to priestly religion.

The message of the social gospel is one of "free religion and political democracy" in opposition to the grasping and oppressive evil of organized groups in society. This view contends that Jesus would have accomplished His purpose under God even without His death. His mission was to "assimilate others to his God–consciousness and to gather a new humanity."[128] He "labored to unite men with God without referring to his death." Had He not run afoul the murderous powers that had determined they could not endure the moral force of His life and teaching, He "would have formed a great society of those who shared his conception and religious realization of God, and this would have been that nucleus of a new humanity which would change the relation of God to humanity."[129]

Though having strong views of the power of the life, words, love, and unintimidated courage of Jesus, Rauschenbusch had virtually no substantial place for the death of Christ. It constituted no effectual part of His purpose. His "God–consciousness" summarized His Sonship. The moral perceptions that caused Him to oppose bigotry, despotism, oppression, religious ritualism, and militaristic nationalism defined His ideas of reconciliation and redemption. This is not the Jesus that Paul knew and preached. This is not the Jesus that Paul admonished Timothy to "remember." Rauschenbusch leads us into a path that is a sure way to forget Jesus Christ.

Shailer Mathews accepted with zeal and aggressive intent the Modernist mantra that "Jesus Christ, the Savior, rather than dogma or even the Bible, is the center of the Modernist's faith."[130] Sans Bible, sans Christian dogma, we have little hope of recognizing the biblical, confessional Jesus "who gave himself for us to redeem us from all lawlessness ... whom He raised from the dead, even Jesus who delivers us from the wrath to come. . . . Christ has redeemed us from the curse of the law, having become a curse for us. . . . In Him we have redemption through His blood, the forgiveness of sins" (Titus 2:14 ESV; 1 Thess. 1:10; Gal. 3:13; Eph. 1:7). Mathews would not give us the Jesus who was "made under the Law, and did perfectly fulfil it and underwent the punishment due to us, which we should have born and suffered, being made Sin and a Curse for us ... by his perfect obedience and sacrifice of himself, which he through the Eternal Spirit once offered up unto God hath fully satisfied the Justice of God, procured reconciliation, and purchased an Everlasting inheritance in the Kingdom of Heaven."[131]

Instead, Mathews showed his unassailable captivity to modern opinions, historicist commitments on religious development, and dismissive attitudes toward historic views of the person and work of Jesus Christ. His survey of "intelligent men" showed that they "do not believe that God's love is limited by the practices of the feudal age, or that it needs to be justified by the sacrifices of the Pagan and Hebrew worlds. They do not consider it worthwhile to consider whether Jesus had one nature or two, one will or two, one person or two." But Mathews was not done with his forsaking of Paul's concerns in order to embrace the concerns of modern "intelligent men." After all, "They are not concerned about his being a ransom to Satan, a satisfaction to divine dignity or a substitutionary victim to divine justice. They cannot use, with any real satisfaction, the theological systems formed of the patterns drawn from politics they have outgrown and repudiated."[132]

Despite Mathews's crafty caricatures and rabid historicism, one can easily see that he lumped biblical views into the same basket with various cultural nuances to relativize the clear apostolic message. "What ever may be the need of humanity," Mathews met the "modern world on its own basis" and does not offer a Christ who is "an archaeological problem or a theological doctrine but a person translatable into influence."[133] A Jesus who can be just anything the modern "intelligent men" want Him to be is not the "Jesus Christ, risen from the dead, the offspring of David, as preached in my gospel."

Just how thoroughly Mathews cleansed salvation of dependence on the substitutionary death of Christ is seen in his explanation of salvation. He claimed that the life and death of Jesus give us entrée into a sphere of "freer individuality." "Salvation is not artificial or judicial. It is an advance in the total personal life made possible by a new and an advanced relationship with the personal God, the way to which is seen in the experience of Jesus." Jesus becomes a phase in human evolution in that His experience "is still a further step in human evolution which has already so largely freed personality from the control of impersonal forces through the working of a fatherly God."[134]

Exactly how "human evolution" has freed humanity from "impersonal forces" Mathews sought to explain in terms of the reports of the resurrection. Some of the reports are likely legendary, he said, but the central fact is one of psychology. "They are historical expressions of the early faith that Jesus had shown himself alive after his passion. And in this faith preserved by the Christian movement [the Modernist] shares."[135] The reports did not show that Jesus actually rose; they did not prove that persons actually saw Him express himself in physical ways in a glorified body; they showed that the early Christians had faith that this had happened; the Christian movement, therefore, is defined by that faith—not any demonstrably necessary historical event. "It is logically inconclusive to say biblical stories are true because the Bible is true," and the faith of the Modernist does not rest upon stories of "eating and drinking, traveling, wounds and disappearances." The Modernist pushes aside these difficulties but still appropriates the "continued influence of the faith of the disciples embodied in the Christian movement."[136] How such dismissal of the resolute conviction of a physical resurrection expressed by the disciples, demonstrated as necessary by Paul in 1 Corinthians 15, and summarized in 2 Timothy 2:8, "risen from the dead," is consistent with "the faith of the disciples" may be insolubly perplexing to the reader. It is to me.

Mathews's theology of the atonement followed the same

contours, dismissing sacrifice as a pattern inherited from pagan and Jewish sources and satisfaction as an objectifying of feudal ideas of honor. That Jesus as God/man was able to render satisfaction to the infinite honor of God, Mathews said, "is clearly derived from feudal ideals and is altogether without biblical support." These ideas were brought over into Protestant confessions in which His death is portrayed as "a satisfaction of divine justice or law . . . a punishment which otherwise would have been borne by humanity itself."[137]

The source for these views was "the new political practices of the days in which the doctrine emerged."[138] So when we summarize what the death of Christ means and strip it of all the culture–bound figures of speech, we affirm that "God shares in human struggles, and that man's progress is not a lonesome search for an unknown God."[139] The corollary events of death and resurrection "help us interpret that long evolutionary struggle from which human life has emerged and which it carries on."[140] Even though the images may be dismissed as morally suspect and as shocking to modern views of justice, they do portray a God whose "salvation never opposes righteousness" and that the "law of sacrifice for ideals is a part of the divine will that is love."[141]

While we may breathe a sigh of relief that Mathews found something commendable in the concept of vicarious atonement, we may be even more amazed and perplexed as to how short he falls of the Pauline admonition, "Remember Jesus Christ."

In a book entitled *As I See Religion,* Harry Emerson Fosdick included a thirty–two–page chapter "What is Christianity?" without any mention of the cross or the death of Christ.[142] In *A Guide to Understanding the Bible,* Fosdick surveyed ancient views, including Old Testament ideas, of substitutionary atonement. The concept of one person suffering for the sins of another and, in so doing, clearing them of the penalty they deserve, "is in view of modern ideas of justice to the individual an immoral outrage."[143] These ideas, alien to modern thought, of "absorption of the individual into the social group" extend all the way to "for as in Adam all die, even so in Christ all shall be made alive" (1 Cor. 15:22). The cross of Christ played a strong role in showing that the purpose of suffering was not to endure a penalty for sin but to call men to "the higher order of self–sacrifice."[144]

Fosdick was fully committed intellectually to the prevailing liberal idea that "static orthodoxies . . . are a menace to the Christian cause."[145] Theology always is shifting and is an exercise in splendid relativism. He affirmed with a vigor worthy of his censorious spirit toward any confidence in propositional revelation but consistent with his faith that "theologies are psychologically and sociologically conditioned and that dogmatism in theology . . . is ridiculous."[146] As applied to the atonement, formulas to explain the death of Christ were "not the everlasting truth they were often taken to be, but were temporary formulations of a great matter, made by men conditioned by their social culture and their psychological reactions to it."[147] Both in the Bible and in historic confessions, therefore, the determining factors were the "legal and penological concepts of the society in which it arose." These theologies seeking coherent explanations of the death of Christ had no claim to absoluteness but, like all theology, "are partial, contemporary attempts to formulate great matters."[148] Don't worry—Fosdick would not make the error of seeking to affirm any abiding truth deduced from biblical propositions.

Fosdick, in spite of relegating every historic "Christian" affirmation to the increasingly large trash heap of relativisms, found a ministry to doctrinally disheveled, discouraged skeptics who were "religiously ruined by such dogmatism"—mainly young people who were "taught to identify the Christian gospel with some sort of orthodoxy" and found that such presentations of the faith were "at war with their intelligence and their Christian experience," and who felt overwhelmed with guilt because of an "unhappy sense of intellectual dishonesty." To the wandering sheep, Fosdick found that his ministry had "been most useful."[149]

If those who have only the light of nature as their source of the knowledge of God and His law are held to be without excuse (Rom. 1:20), how much more culpable are those who hear and are taught with earnestness about the blood of redemption shed on the cross and count it as nothing. Scripture says with clarity and with a perfect persuasion of its truthfulness that "a death has occurred that redeems them from the transgressions committed under the first covenant" (Heb. 9:15 ESV). How can such men hold these positions without an aggressive denial of the inspiration and revelatory truthfulness of the Bible and its teaching about the propitiatory, substitutionary character of the cross? A severe warning of "worse punishment" is given to one who "has trampled underfoot the Son of God" by denying His intrinsic, essential deity as the eternal Son of the Father, "and has profaned the blood of the covenant" by denying its eternal purpose and its efficacy for the forgiveness of transgressions, and has "outraged the Spirit of grace" by denying His personal role in bringing Christ unblemished from birth to the point of shedding His blood for the remission of sins (Heb. 10:29; 9:14 ESV). Those who championed themselves as having salvaged Christianity for the cultured intellectuals of the day have proved to be among those of whom Paul wrote, "If we deny Him, He also will deny us. If we are faithless, He remains faithful; He cannot deny Himself" (2 Tim. 2:12–13).

18

A Concluding Reflection

The terse summary of Christian truth commended by Paul to Timothy in 2 Timothy 2:8 as a summary of his eternal privilege in ministry gives us a call to embrace wholeheartedly the entire spectrum of gospel life. It shows that believers are the recipients of the promises contained in an eternal covenant. It shows the infinite wonder of the Person in whom the triune God has secured these covenant blessings. It sets before us the lovely life of Jesus and draws us to His humble condescension, His gracious emptying, and allows us to sit with comfort and security at His feet for instruction and grace to help us. It points us to the cross where this humble person, out of a capacity for endurance hidden from His contemporaries, bore the eternal wrath of the holy and mighty God justly imposed on Him as our propitiatory substitute. It shows us the splendor of His deity, His intrinsic as well as His merited lordship, and His triumph over death in a complete victory for his chosen people so that the grave has lost its power to intimidate. It shows us the righteousness of the law of God as an expression of His holy character, His exclusive prerogative, and His eternal justice. It shows us that Christ is made "to us wisdom from God, and righteousness and sanctification, and redemption" (1 Cor. 1:30 NASB). It bows us in pure and joyful worship before the God of heaven and earth, the God of purity, holiness, righteousness, justice, patience, lovingkindness, mercy, forgiveness, reconciliation, redemption, and grace, the God who inhabits eternity and in whom we live and move and have our being, and who has "rescued us from the domain of darkness, and transferred us to the kingdom of His beloved Son" (Col. 1:13 NASB).

The Liberal reinterpretation of Christianity intent on salvaging Christianity instead engaged in its destruction. "The real office of formula is to help an age make the experience of salvation intelligible and consistently tenable," as Shailer Mathews put it. The way in which the Liberals would "help an age" see salvation as tenable was to present Jesus as "the immanent Spiritual Life of God localized in a human personality."[150] In giving credibility of this sort to their age, we were taught to forget Genesis 1:1 about God's fiat creation, to forget Genesis 1:26 about the special creation of man and woman immediately in the image of God, and to forget Genesis 3 concerning a space–time fall of humanity in our first parents, specifically in Adam's transgression. We were taught to ignore Luke 1:35 and its virgin conception of a child who would be both the eternal Son and conceived man. The entire event was supposedly a fable derived from an ignorant worldview; we were thus given a Christ who was only a man. We were taught to ignore Romans 4:23–25 and 2 Corinthians 5:21 because the whole system of imputation is a moral outrage. We were taught to discount by one hundred percent Ephesians 1:7 because redemption has nothing to do with the shedding of blood, forgiveness, or grace. We were taught that social action in the present age is superior to any concern about personal salvation in eternity. We were taught that knowledge of God is not found in the propositions of Scripture as an inspired revelation from God and that we could track Jesus's consciousness of His Sonship and find that our growing consciousness of our being sons of God could duplicate His.

Liberals ruined the "mainline" denominations with their radical skepticism disguised as piety. They eviscerated their missions, destroyed their evangelism, turned their preaching into psychological counseling, and made human consciousness the final criterion for truth. They trained their generation, and bequeathed to the following generations, a culture void of any redemptive message or true moral guidance. Human consciousness was absolutized—the generations learned the lesson well. People can now be any gender they feel like being, establish any morality that seems appealing, and embrace any ideas as truth for them. They created both the listlessness and the lawlessness that plagues American society.

Liberals were concerned that they could not generate the kind of enthusiasm for Christian faith or ideals that was produced by the conservative, Bible–believing, individualistic Christianity of historic orthodoxy. Shailer Mathews's criticism of conservatives was set in the context of a wistful appreciation of their driving and sincere spirituality. "Yet there are thousands of men and women of noblest Christian character," he recognized, "of splendid moral enthusiasm and religious earnestness, who believe in a hell of literal fire, in a personal devil, in demoniacal possession, in the absolute inerrancy of all the Biblical writings, in the creation of the world in six days, in the physical coming of Christ in the sky, and in the materialistic resurrection of the body through a miraculous recombination of its original or other particles." He marveled that any could hold such ideas in the modern word; these people, religiously and philosophically, "are to all intents and purposes citizens of the first century of our era." They are "contemporary but not modern." Their views "imply an abandonment of the modern world as constituted by science." When one considers, however, the overall purpose of religion, "no serious thinker can fail to respect such loyalty to a literalistic gospel or to seek to emulate the *earnest religion it engenders*."[151]

Walter Rauschenbusch recognized that his way of viewing the "gospel" would have to build a new road to such apparent piety and devotion. "The only question is whether we can win just as strong a sense of the presence of God from this complicated social process of inspiration, as when God was believed to have dictated the books by a psychological miracle." Inspiration did not come from a divinely initiated source but from inward perceptions that were personally generated. Establishing a sense of devotion to the ideas thus proposed will take time, intellectual energy, and patience.

"It can be done," he assured his readers, "but the interpreter needs personal acquaintance with inspiration to do it."[152] One is forced to ask, with little confidence of any workable, objective, transferable, publicly recognizable product of such inspiration, "To whose ideas are we to give credence, and what are the reasons why?"

Jonathan Edwards wrote about the source of this earnestness and "strong sense of the presence of God" in *Religious Affections*. He placed all true religion within the framework of affections and gave this explanation of the relation between human consciousness and objective reality.

> The Apostle seems to make a distinction between mere speculative knowledge of the things of religion, and spiritual knowledge. . . . When the true beauty and amiableness of the holiness or true moral good that is in divine things, is discovered to the soul, it as it were opens a new world to its view. . . . the glorifying of God's moral perfections, is the special end of all the works of God's hands. By this sense of the moral beauty of divine things, is understood the sufficiency of Christ as a mediator: for 'tis only by the discovery of the beauty of the moral perfection of Christ that the believer is let into the knowledge of the excellency of his person, so as to know anything more of it than the devils do: and 'tis only by the knowledge of the excellency of Christ's person, that any know his sufficiency as a mediator; for the latter depends upon, and arises from the former. 'Tis by seeing the excellency of Christ's person, that the saints are made

sensible of the preciousness of his blood, and its sufficiency to atone for sin: for therein consists the preciousness of Christ's blood, that 'tis the blood of so excellent and amiable a person. And on this depends the meritoriousness of his obedience, and sufficiency and prevalence of his intercession. By this sight of the moral beauty of divine things, is seen the beauty of the way of salvation by Christ: for that consists in the beauty of the moral perfections of God, which wonderfully shines forth in every step of this method of salvation, from beginning to end. By this is seen the fitness and suitableness of this way: for this wholly consists in its tendency to deliver us from sin and hell, and to bring us to the happiness which consists in the possession and enjoyment of moral good, in a way sweetly agreeing with God's moral perfections. And in the way's being contrived so as to attain these ends, consists the excellent wisdom of that way. By this is seen the excellency of the Word of God: take away all the moral beauty and sweetness in the Word, and the Bible is left wholly a dead letter, a dry, lifeless, tasteless thing. By this is seen the true foundation of our duty; the worthiness of God to be so esteemed, honored, loved, submitted to, and served, as he requires of us, and the amiableness of the duties themselves that are required of us.[153]

With this description of the compelling wonder of God, Christ, Scripture, atonement, heaven, and obedient service to God, one may savor the grace contained in Paul's admonition: "Remember Jesus Christ, risen from the dead, the offspring of David, as preached in my gospel" (2 Tim. 2:8 ESV).

Precisely the absence of all of these grippingly beautiful perfections made Liberalism itself a dead letter for Christianity and a destructive force in culture. Liberals repudiated the beauty and excellence of the Word of God and thus had no authority by which to show the moral perfection and infinite wonder of God's wisdom. They culled and pared at biblical orthodoxy on Christ's person to make worship of Him an act of idolatry. They eliminated wrath, hell, the legitimacy of divine determination to punish transgression, and the necessity of an interpositional rescue so that the cross fizzled as a focus of forgiven sin, infinite mercy, culminating grace, eternal love, and a Savior's act of perfect obedience. They forgot everything and made Christian faith a path to destruction.

The past, the present, the future, freedom from the pervasively destructive ugliness of sin, the perfect clarity and substantial reification of truth, the vanishing of error, living in the presence of holiness in saints, the ever–increasing delight of the unchanging beauty of God, and experiencing the transforming power of a vision of Christ as He reflects in His person and consummated work the eternal wisdom of God—all these blessings and more come from this simple command: "Remember Jesus Christ."

Endnotes

[1] John Calvin, *Calvin's New Testament Commentaries, Volume 10: 2 Corinthians and Timothy, Titus, & Philemon* (Grand Rapids, MI: Eerdmans), 311.

[2] Calvin, *New Testament Commentaries, Volume 10*, 311.

[3] Michael Holmes, ed., *The Apostolic Fathers*, second edition, (Grand Rapids, MI: Baker, 1991), 53.

[4] Holmes, *The Apostolic Fathers*, 55.

[5] Holmes, *The Apostolic Fathers*, 29.

[6] Holmes, *The Apostolic Fathers*, 32.

[7] Holmes, *The Apostolic Fathers*, 35.

[8] Holmes, *The Apostolic Fathers*, 36.

[9] Holmes, *The Apostolic Fathers*, 37–38.

[10] Holmes, *The Apostolic Fathers*, 42.

[11] Holmes, *The Apostolic Fathers*, 45.

[12] Holmes, *The Apostolic Fathers*, 48.

[13] Holmes, *The Apostolic Fathers*, 56.

[14] Holmes, *The Apostolic Fathers*, 51.

[15] Holmes, *The Apostolic Fathers*, 59.

[16] Holmes, *The Apostolic Fathers*, 53.

[17] Holmes, *The Apostolic Fathers*, 57.

[18] Holmes, *The Apostolic Fathers*, 40.

[19] Holmes, *The Apostolic Fathers*, 56.

[20] This word, similar to the Latin *circumincessio*, means that all three persons of the Trinity are involved together in every divine action in ways fitting to their inter–personal relations. An English word used to identify this doctrine is "coinherence."

[21] Holmes, *The Apostolic Fathers*, 61.

[22] Holmes, *The Apostolic Fathers*, 61.

[23] Holmes, *The Apostolic Fathers*, 63.

[24] Holmes, *The Apostolic Fathers*, 64.

[25] Holmes, *The Apostolic Fathers*, 88.

[26] Holmes, *The Apostolic Fathers*, 88.

[27] Holmes, *The Apostolic Fathers*, 92.

[28] Holmes, *The Apostolic Fathers*, 100.

[29] Justin Martyr, *St. Justin Martyr: The First and Second Apologies*, trans. Leslie William Barnard (New York: Paulist Press, 1997), 44, 46, 84.

[30] Irenaeus, *Against Heresies*, I:x:1.

[31] Irenaeus, *Against Heresies*, V.xx.2

[32] Tertullian, *Prescription Against Heretics*, 13.

[33] *The Works of St. Augustine: On Christian Belief* (New York: New City Press, 2005), 275 (emphasis original).

[34] A. T. Robertson, *Word Pictures in the New Testament*, 6 vols., (Grand Rapids, MI: Baker Book House, 1932), 5:4.

[35] Edward R. Hardy, *Christology of the Later Fathers* (Louisville: Westminster John Knox Press, 1954) 329, 330.

[36] My translation, from Philip Schaff, *Creeds of Christendom*, 3 vols., (Grand Rapids: Baker Book House, 1919), 2:60

[37] Athanasius, *On the Incarnation of the Word*, ch. 4.

[38] Athanasius, *Contra Arianos*, III.63.

[39] Athanasius, *Contra Arianos*, III. xxiii.4

[40] Hardy, *Christology of the Later Fathers*, 353

[41] Hardy, *Christology of the Later Fathers*, 368.

[42] Hardy, *Christology of the Later Fathers*, 359.

[43] Hardy, *Christology of the Later Fathers*, 359–370.

[44] Hardy, *Christology of the Later Fathers,* 366.

[45] John A. Broadus, *Commentary on the Gospel of Matthew*, (Philadelphia: American Baptist Publication Society, 1886), 493.

[46] Philip Schaff, *The Creeds of Christendom*, 2:62, 63.

[47] William Lumpkin, *Baptist Confessions of Faith*, (King of Prussia: Judson Press, 1959), 160.

[48] Shailer Mathews, *New Faith for Old: An Autobiography* (New York: The MacMillan Company, 1936), 286–287.

[49] Shailer Mathews, *The Faith of Modernism* (New York: The Macmillan Company, 1925), 13.

[50] Mathews, *The Faith of Modernism*, 22.

[51] Mathews, *The Faith of Modernism*, 27.

[52] Mathews, *The Faith of Modernism*, 19.

[53] William Newton Clarke, *Sixty Years with the Bible: A Record of Experience* (New York: Charles Scribner's Sons, 1909), 219.

[54] Clarke, *Sixty Years*, 219.

[55] William Newton Clarke, *The Use of the Scriptures in Theology* (New York: Charles Scribner's Sons, 1906), 219.

[56] William Newton Clarke, *An Outline of Christian Theology* (New York: Charles Scribner's Sons, 1922), 20.

[57] Clarke, *Outline,* 36.

[58] Clarke, *Outline,* 36

[59] Walter Rauschenbusch, *A Theology for the Social Gospel* (New York: The Macmillan Company, 1922), 21, 147. The original copyright is 1917, one year before Rauschenbusch's death.

[60] Mathews, *The Faith of Modernism*, 38.

[61] Mathews, *The Faith of Modernism*, 43.

[62] Mathews, *The Faith of Modernism*, 47.

[63] Mathews, *The Faith of Modernism*, 52.

[64] Mathews, *The Faith of Modernism*, 52.

[65] Mathews, *The Faith of Modernism*, 50.

[66] Mathews, *The Faith of Modernism*, 47.

[67] Mathews, *The Faith of Modernism*, 53.

[68] Harry Emerson Fosdick, *The Living of These Days* (New York: Harper & Brothers, 1956), 52.

[69] Clarke, *Sixty Years*, 107–108

[70] Clarke, *Sixty Years*, 210–211 (emphasis added).

[71] Clarke, *The Use of the Scriptures*, 27.

[72] I capitalize Liberal, Liberalism, Liberals to identify this group as a distinct and recognizable entity maintaining a distinct worldview and disguising their doctrinal infidelity as a Christianity credible and appealing to modern naturalism and historicism. This distinguishes it from the use of the word liberal as meaning a fair–minded and congenial individual.

[73] Friedrich Schleiermacher, *The Christian Faith*, (Edinburgh: T & T Clark, 1989), 382.

[74] Schleiermacher, *The Christian Faith*, 382.

[75] Schleiermacher, *The Christian Faith*, 385.

[76] David Friedrich Strauss, *Strauss' Life of Jesus, Volume One*, trans. George Eliot (New York: Gloger Family Books. 1993), 130, 177.

[77] William Newton Clarke, *What Shall We Think of Christianity?* (New York: Charles Scribner's Sons, 1900), 70.

[78] Clarke, *What Shall We Think of Christianity?*, 71.

[79] Clarke, *Outline*, 297–298.

[80] Clarke, *Outline*, 333.

[81] Clarke, *What Shall We Think of Christianity?* 51–53.

[82] Clarke, *What Shall We Think of Christianity?* 51–53.

[83] Rauschenbusch, *A Theology*, 191.

[84] Rauschenbusch, *A Theology*, 193.

[85] Rauschenbusch, *A Theology*, 195.

[86] Rauschenbusch, *A Theology*, 25.

[87] Rauschenbusch, *A Theology*, 154–155.

[88] Mathews, *New Faith for Old*, 70.

[89] Mathews, *New Faith for Old*, 231.

[90] Mathews, *The Faith of Modernism*, 83.

[91] Mathews, *The Faith of Modernism*, 138.

[92] Mathews, *The Faith of Modernism*, 142.

[93] Mathews, *The Faith of Modernism*, 124, 133.

[94] Mathews, *The Faith of Modernism*, 136.

[95] Mathews, *The Faith of Modernism*, 136.

[96] Mathews, *The Faith of Modernism*, 137–138.

[97] Mathews, *The Faith of Modernism*, 142.

[98] Mathews, *The Faith of Modernism*, 143.

[99] Rauschenbusch, *A Theology*, 149–152.

[100] Rauschenbusch, *A Theology*, 150.

[101] Rauschenbusch, *A Theology*, 217.

[102] Rauschenbusch, *A Theology*, 153.

[103] Tom J. Nettles, The Baptists, 3 vols (Fearn, Ross–shire, Scotland: Christian Focus Publications, 2007) 3:149–150.

[104] William Newton Clarke, *Commentary on the Gospel of Mark* in *An American Commentary on the New Testament,* ed. Alvah Hovey, (Valley Forge: Judson Press, 1881), 243–244.

[105] Clarke, *Commentary on the Gospel of Mark*, 243–244.

[106] Clarke, *Commentary on the Gospel of Mark*, 243–244.

[107] Clarke, *Outline*, 352.

108 Clarke, *Outline*, 338.

109 Clarke, *Outline,* 330.

110 Clarke, *Outline,* 331.

111 Clarke, *Outline,* 333.

112 Clarke, *Outline,* 349.

113 Clarke, *Outline,* 347.

114 Clarke, *Outline,* 347.

115 Clarke, *Outline,* 471.

116 Clarke, *Outline,* 347.

117 Clarke, *Outline,* 452, 475, 477.

118 Rauschenbusch, *Theology*, 244.

119 Rauschenbusch, *Theology*, 244.

120 Rauschenbusch, *Theology*, 243, 245.

121 Rauschenbusch, *Theology*, 242.

122 Rauschenbusch, *Theology*, 247.

123 Rauschenbusch, *Theology*, 258.

124 Rauschenbusch, *Theology*, 259.

125 Rauschenbusch, *Theology*, 260.

126 Rauschenbusch, *Theology*, 261.

127 Rauschenbusch, *Theology*, 262, 274–279.

128 Rauschenbusch, *Theology*, 266.

129 Rauschenbusch, *Theology*, 266.

130 Mathews, *The Faith of Modernism*, 144.

131 Second London Baptist Confession, Chapter 8, Paragraphs 4–5.

132 Mathews, *The Faith of Modernism,* 146.

133 Mathews, *The Faith of Modernism,* 146

134 Mathews, *The Faith of Modernism*, 152.

[135] Mathews, *The Faith of Modernism*, 153.

[136] Mathews, *The Faith of Modernism*, 155.

[137] Mathews, *The Faith of Modernism*, 157.

[138] Mathews, *The Faith of Modernism*, 157.

[139] Mathews, *The Faith of Modernism*, 160.

[140] Mathews, *The Faith of Modernism*, 161.

[141] Mathews, *The Faith of Modernism*, 159, 161.

[142] Harry Emerson Fosdick, *As I See Religion* (New York: Harper and Brothers, 1932), 32–63. In that chapter, Fosdick expanded his thesis that "the genius of Christianity lies in reverence for personality." He wrote, "Whether one really is a Christian or not depends on whether one accepts or rejects Jesus' attitude toward personality," 43.

[143] Harry Emerson Fosdick, *A Guide to Understanding the Bible* (New York: Harper and Brothers Publishers, 1938), 59.

[144] Fosdick, *A Guide to Understanding the Bible*, 199.

[145] Harry Emerson Fosdick, *The Living of These Days* (New York: Harper & Brothers, 1956), 230.

[146] Fosdick, *The Living of These Days*, 231.

[147] Fosdick, *The Living of These Days*, 232.

[148] Fosdick, *The Living of These Days*, 232.

[149] Fosdick, *The Living of These Days*, 233.

[150] Shailer Mathews, *The Gospel and the Modern Man* (New York: The Macmillan Company, 1910), 137–138.

[151] Mathews, *The Gospel and the Modern Man*, 69–70 (emphasis added).

[152] Rauschenbusch, *A Theology*, 191.

[153] Jonathan Edwards, *Religious Affections*, ed. John E. Smith (New Haven: Yale University Press, 1959), 272–274. This was first published in 1746 in Boston. This is volume 2 of the Yale edition of *The Works of Jonathan Edwards*.

Scripture Index

Old Testament

FOUNDERS

M I N I S T R I E S

Founders Ministries exists for the recovery of the gospel and the reformation of churches.

We have been providing resources for churches since 1982 through conferences, books, *The Sword & The Trowel Podcast*, video documentaries, online articles found at www. founders.org, the quarterly *Founders Journal*, Bible studies, International church search, and the seminary level training program, the Institute of Public Theology. Founders believes that the biblical faith is inherently doctrinal, and we are therefore confessional in our convictions.

You can learn more about Founders Ministries and how to partner with us at www.founders.org.

 FoundersMin

 FoundersMin

 FoundersMinistries

 FoundersMinistries

Other Titles from Founders Press

Serious Joy: Reflections and Devotions on Jonathan Edwards' Seventy Resolutions
By Joey Tomlinson

Joey Tomlinson has written a wonderful introduction and guide to Edwards' Resolutions, wisely expounding and pressing them into the corners of our lives. I'm glad to commend this little book in *Serious Joy*.

—Joe Rigney, Fellow of
Theology,
New Saint Andrews College

To the Judicious and Impartial Reader: Baptist Symbolics Volume 2
By James Renihan

This work should be a consistently consulted treasure of truth-centered theological instruction and grace-centered, Christ centered, God-centered spiritual formation.

—Tom Nettles,
Senior Professor of Historical Theology,
The Southern Baptist Theological Seminary
Founding Faculty, Institute of Public Theology

For the Vindication of the Truth: Baptist Symbolics Volume 1
By James Renihan

I have longed to see a critical exposition of the First London Confession of Faith in print, one that provides a detailed examination of the provenance, structure, theology, editions, and impact of this notable text. This is that!

—Michael A. G. Haykin,
Chair & Professor,
The Southern Baptist Theological Seminary

Truth & Grace Memory Books
Edited by Thomas K. Ascol

Memorizing a good, age-appropriate catechism is as valuable
for learning the Bible as memorizing multiplication tables is
for learning mathematics.

—Dr. Don Whitney,
Professor,
The Southern Baptist Theological Seminary

Dear Timothy: Letters on Pastoral Ministry
Edited by Thomas K. Ascol

Get this book. So many experienced pastors have written in
this book it is a gold mine of wisdom for young pastors in
how to preach and carry out their ministerial life.

—Joel Eeeke, President,
Puritan Reformed Theological Seminary

The Mystery of Christ, His Covenant & His Kingdom
By Samuel Renihan

This book serves for an excellent and rich primer on covenant
theology and demonstrates how it leads from the Covenant
of Redemption to the final claiming and purifying of the
people given by the Father to the Son.

—Tom Nettles,
Senior Professor of Historical Theology,
The Southern Baptist Theological Seminary
Founding Faculty, Institute of Public Theology

Additional titles

A Primer for Conflict
By Josh Howard

Missions by the Book: How Theology and Missions Walk Together
By Chad Vegas and Alex Kocman

*Still Confessing:
An Exposition of the Baptist Faith & Message 2000*
By Daniel Scheiderer

By His Grace and for His Glory
By Tom Nettles

Getting the Garden Right
By Richard C. Barcellos

The Law and the Gospel
By Ernie Reisinger

Teaching Truth, Training Hearts
By Tom Nettles

Just Thinking: about the state
By Darrell Harrison and Virgil Walker

The Transcultural Gospel
By E.D. Burns

Ancient Gospel, Brave New World
By E.D. Burns

Order these titles and more at press.founders.org